Let God Guide You Daily

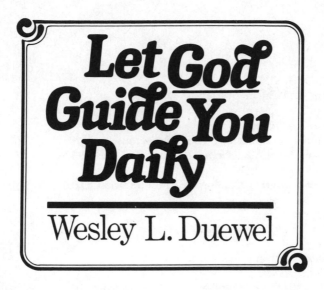

Let God Guide You Daily

Wesley L. Duewel

Foreword by George Verwer

FRANCIS ASBURY PRESS
of Zondervan Publishing House
Grand Rapids. Michigan

LET GOD GUIDE YOU DAILY
Copyright © 1988 by Wesley L. Duewel

FRANCIS ASBURY PRESS
is an imprint of Zondervan Publishing House,
1415 Lake Drive, S.E., Grand Rapids, Michigan 49506.

Library of Congress Cataloging in Publication Data

Duewel, Wesley L.
    Let God guide you daily.

    Bibliography: p.
    Includes index.
    1. Christian life—1960–   . 2. Providence and government of
God. I. Title.
bV4501.2.D737   1988   248.4   87-33371
ISBN 0-310-36171-0

Printed in the United States of America

88 89 90 91 92 93 / AF / 10 9 8 7 6 5 4 3 2 1

To John, Christine, and Darlene
Praying that God will guide you always

acknowledgments

To my wife, Betty, for her patience during my long hours in the office, and to Hilda Johnecheck, my secretary, for the hours spent on this manuscript

contents

fOREWORd

Are you experiencing God's guidance daily? A high percentage of Christians are missing God's best for their lives. That is one of the reasons why this book by Dr. Wesley Duewel is so important. Take time to read it prayerfully and carefully.

Learning how to discern God's guidance daily is something that we must learn out on God's marathon running track. That track is paved with forgiveness. I believe the glue that helps hold together the whole challenge of God's guidance and will is forgiveness. We need to understand in depth how God can forgive us again and again. Don't be discouraged if you think you have missed part of God's plan for your life. By faith bounce back into the battle and keep your eyes on the Lord.

Let God Guide You Daily is written on the foundation of the Word of God. It would be good to look up the passages of Scripture as you read through the book.

Wesley Duewel was one of the very first missionaries I met when I went to India, and I have had the privilege of knowing him for more than twenty-five years. He is a person who has put into practice the principles that he describes in this book.

It is my prayer that this powerful book will help you discover God's guidance again and again. Then you will have a fruitful and powerful walk with the Lord.

George Verwer
Founder-President,
Operation Mobilization

preface

God desires to make His guidance a natural part of your daily life, so natural that you learn to relax in His faithfulness and often experience His guiding hand almost without realizing it. He wants it to be part of His daily goodness to you, His daily help for you. It is His gift of love to you.

Guidance is your privilege as a child of God. It can become a daily joy and thrill as part of your spiritual lifestyle. The term "will of God" seems awesome and almost frightening to many people. Let's emphasize experiencing God's guiding hand, and as we do we will be living in the will of God.

I wrote this book with the prayer that through it you will find God's guidance beautifully simple. God does not want it to seem complicated to you. It is His loving provision to help you be at your best in effective living.

How dare I write a book on guidance when I still have so much for the Holy Spirit to teach me? I recognize that I am only learning the ABC's of many aspects of prayer, guidance, and the beautiful fruit of the Spirit. But I have felt urged—yes, compelled—by the Spirit to prepare this book. I want you, too, to discover the joy of daily guidance. Pray that I, too, may be an example of the guided life.

Wesley L. Duewel

1

GUIDANCE IS FOR YOU

Guidance is for you! The guided life can be your joyous daily experience. God is interested in all your life. He is glad to guide you in the special crisis moments. He is equally glad to make your daily living preciously sacred by repeated moments of guidance in your ordinary situations. Guidance is for you day by day. Let me share with you how blessed your experience can be.

Guidance Is Your Privilege

I have a deep conviction that you and I are living far removed from the privileges God has prepared for us. Too many people seem unconvinced that God seriously desires to guide them daily in their practical living.

One minister friend said, "Oh, don't you think guidance is a rather dangerous subject? People get impressionistic!" It is true that there can be an unwholesome emphasis on impressions. God wants us to distinguish between His guidance and other impressions. Another young minister said to me, "Why, I would never think of asking God to guide me in a thing like marriage. I believe God just expects us to use our common sense." As if common sense left us when God guides us!

God's Word has an amazing abundance of examples, promises, and truths related to guidance. Why are we so silent on this subject? Is Satan trying to close our mouths and rob us of God's plan for our lives? Is he afraid of what will happen if God's people really take guidance seriously?

The biographies of God's saints are filled with thrilling accounts of God's clear guidance. Church history bears witness that God has led not only individuals but also entire groups of people. God has led to issue calls to prayer for revival and then sent mighty outpourings of His Spirit. He has led peoples to pray for protection in time of war and has sent miracle answers to groups and nations. He has led to call for prayer for rain, and drought has been broken. God has led committees in discussion until, in their decisions, they could say with the early church, "It seemed good to the Holy Spirit and to us" (Acts 15:28).

Everybody Wants Guidance

There is widespread secular interest in illicit forms of guidance. Why do many desire hidden information about the future? Horoscopes, tarot cards, tea leaves, Ouija boards, séances, and other forms of occult guidance are contrary to Bible teaching. God condemned Saul to death for seeking illicit means of guidance (1 Chron. 10:13–14). Yet He gave great details of guidance to David when he sought God's will.

We are living in an age that depends on counselors. Almost every aspect of life and work is now aided by professionally trained specialists called counselors: health, psychology, education, management, and almost every area of business and industry.

Thank God for all the skills that have been developed in this important field. It has taken us thousands of years to realize the importance that God from the beginning has placed on counseling. One of the great names prophesied for Jesus by Isaiah was "Wonderful Counselor" (Isa. 9:6). God knows you need divine counsel.

Let me encourage you to expect a new, thrilling joy as you begin to put God's guidance into your daily experience. It is sacredly precious to learn to discern the gentle guidance of the Spirit. Read on and trust God to begin to guide you more fully from this day forward.

2

expect god to guide you

Is it really true that "the LORD will guide you always" (Isa. 58:11)? Can you truthfully say that daily guidance is your experience? The New American Standard Bible translates the verse, "The LORD will continually guide you." Is God's guidance so continuous that it has become the habit of your spiritual walk with God?

Guidance is to be one of the marks that distinguish you as a child of God, because "those who are led by the Spirit of God are sons of God" (Rom. 8:14). God wants you to have joyful assurance that He is leading you. He is giving you purpose in life and a destiny in your future. By this He adds direction and significance to your life. Are you hungry to know this increasingly in your own experience?

Because God Is Your Father

Because God is truly your Father, you can expect to rely on His Fatherhood constantly. What are the two most common ways God benefits you daily with His Fatherhood? Obviously, by His help and by His guidance. As your Father, He does not intrude into your life; He does not dominate you so that your own initiative and freedom of choice are infringed. But always and in every situation He is available to you in all His Fatherhood.

Your longing to know God's will, to be led by Him, is His gift to you. His Holy Spirit in your heart creates and deepens this desire. Your longing testifies to His infinitely deeper desire to guide you. He wants you to experience all He is planning for you.

There is no way you can maximize your life except as God guides. So He gave you the desire to know what is best. God did not give this hunger to mock you. He plans to satisfy it just as He plans to satisfy your every holy desire.

God knows the beautiful plans He has for you, what your immediate future holds, and the total situation before you. He enjoys guiding you; He is deeply satisfied every time you turn to Him. He has great joy in being a Father to you. He wants it to become normal that you constantly turn to Him for guidance.

Because Jesus Is Your Shepherd

Twice Jesus said that He was the Good Shepherd (John 10:11, 14). It is normal for a shepherd to guide. It is as normal to lead as it is to feed, protect, or provide rest for the sheep. Walking with Jesus, the Good Shepherd, is to walk in guidance, to be led by Jesus. This is so normal to a sheep that it hardly realizes it is being led by the shepherd. Jesus wants it to become so normal to you that you often scarcely realize how much you are being led.

Because the Spirit Is Your Counselor

The Holy Spirit indwells you to be your special Counselor. If Jesus were visibly by your side, He would be your constant Counselor. Since He returned to the Father, He made the Holy Spirit His provision for you. "I will ask the Father, and he will give you another Counselor to be with you forever. . . . you know him, for he lives with you and will be in you" (John 14:16–17).

Because Guidance Can Be Normal

It is one of the Holy Spirit's special, continuous roles to be your Counselor. How will He counsel you? Sometimes He may speak through special means—through a vision, dream, or audible voice. But this will be rare. God used those methods more in Old Testament times before people had Bibles. God nowhere promises to speak to you in this way. If He so chooses, He is free to do so—but you should not ask for it or expect it.

God wants to speak to you in a far more natural, normal way.

How? Jesus says of the Spirit, "You know him, for he lives with you and will be in you" (John 14:17). Can you really say that you know the Holy Spirit? Jesus wants you to know the Spirit as the most normal, constant Counselor of your life. He wants you to be filled with the Spirit, led by the Spirit, assisted in your prayer by the Spirit, empowered by the Spirit, and kept cleansed and victorious by the Spirit. And all this is to be so natural and normal to you that it is interwoven in all your life.

The Counselor

Before the Cross, during His last hours with His disciples in the Upper Room, Jesus gave some of the deepest teaching of His ministry. He spoke in new clarity and detail about the fuller role the Holy Spirit would assume after He Himself ascended to the Father. And His favorite term then for the Spirit was not "the Cleanser," "the Empowerer," "the Baptizer," "the Anointer," or even "the Teacher." It was "the Counselor."

Jesus clearly expected counseling or guidance to be a major role of the Holy Spirit to you as a Spirit-filled believer. He desired that your life be a guided life, constantly led by the Spirit.

3

GOD'S GREAT PLAN FOR YOU

God delights to plan for His children. No human father ever experienced such joy in planning for his child as God experiences as He plans for you. He does not want you to miss any part of His beautiful purpose for you. His plans are filled with details of blessing, joy, and wonderful surprises. David said, "The things you planned for us no one can recount to you; were I to speak and tell of them, they would be too many to declare" (Ps. 40:5).

God's plans for you are not static. If you have missed part of His plan for you, He is still eager to begin where you are today and adapt His plans to the best possible sequence from where you are now. As a father adapts his planning to the changing needs of his child, so God coordinates His planning with the realities of your life. If you make one mistake, this does not destroy all God's purpose for you. Be of good courage; God has not stopped His planning for you. He instantly adapts to your needs.

Never become discouraged. Sometime you may realize that you have failed to seek God's guidance or have failed to interpret His will properly. Do not spend a long time mourning. Ask God's forgiveness and go on with your life and ministry, just as David did.

Anyone can make a mistake; anyone can miss God's will in some decision or action. But how wonderful that God is so loving, merciful, and understanding! "As a father has compassion on his children, so the LORD has compassion on those who fear him; for he knows how we are formed, he remembers that we are dust" (Ps. 103:13–14). God can overrule your failure or mistake. "I will repay you for the years the locusts have eaten," God said through Joel (2:25).

No mistake is so serious but that God can start anew and make something worthwhile from your life. It is said that in making a Persian rug the master weaver stands on one side of the loom and shouts instructions to the small boys weaving on the other side. If a boy should make a serious mistake, a truly great master weaver can weave the boy's error into the pattern and others will never realize a mistake was made. God is far greater than any master weaver. God can take any surrendered life and even weave our mistakes into something useful and beautiful.

God's word to Israel through Jeremiah was, "I know the plans I have for you, . . . plans to prosper you, ...plans to give you hope and a future" (Jer. 29:11). Note that *plans* is in the plural. Though this promise was originally given to Israel, it contains spiritual truth for you and me too. This is typical of God. He is a God of constant planning and of multiple plans for everyone. He plans not only for your spiritual welfare, but also for your home life, your work, your financial future—in fact, for all your needs. Is not that the meaning of Philippians 4:19: "My God will meet all your needs"?

Because God constantly thinks of you, loves you, and plans for you, you are in constant need of His guiding help so that you get the full benefits and blessings of all His plans.

1. God's guidance is the only way to be sure of the maximum investment of your life. God's overall, eternal plan will eventually prevail. He makes His plan for you in the light of His plan for the whole universe, in the light of His plans for time and eternity. What a fool you would be to fail to make full use of God's planning for you, to fail to relate to and build into His plan, which will eventually prevail.

God alone sees what is best for you, your family, God's people, and the world. How little you realize what influence your life can have when you are in the will of God! How little did Stephen realize that God would use his martyrdom to help win Paul and thus influence the whole Christian world!

When the Spirit directed Philip to leave the tremendous revival God had sent to Samaria through him, it did not seem logical. God had been using him mightily in Samaria. Crowds gathered to hear him, turned to the Lord, and were baptized (Acts 8). God used Philip to perform miraculous signs, to heal the sick, and to cast out evil spirits. The whole city was stirred, and "there was great joy" in this first revival after Pentecost (v. 8). So great was the movement of God's Spirit that the group of apostles at Jerusalem sent Peter and John to help, and many were filled with the Spirit. Then Peter and John returned to Jerusalem and left the work in Philip's hands.

Now suddenly the Holy Spirit told Philip to go to the desert road that led to Gaza. He had to travel thirty-five miles to Jerusalem and then take the nearly sixty-mile desert road to Gaza, the southernmost city of Palestine on the border of Egypt. Humanly speaking, this did not make sense, but Philip obeyed. Through the Ethiopian eunuch won by Philip on that hot, dusty road, God opened Africa to the gospel. Through the conversion of this state treasurer, probably more people were won to Christ than through all the rest of Philip's ministry.

2. God's guidance adds dignity, eternal value, and glory to your life. You become an important element in God's overall plan. If you miss God's guidance, you may be forgotten in eternity.

How little did the Reverend Mordecai Ham realize when God guided him to evangelistic meetings in Charlotte, North Carolina, that God would save Billy Graham and through him touch millions of lives!

3. God's guidance is the only way that guarantees eternal success. Jonah tried to run away from God and found he could not. Jezebel tried to avoid God's will and God's prophet, but she left her name as a curse word over the ages. No one can succeed in resisting God's will. God's plan will prevail. You will succeed when you fit into His plan.

The LORD foils the plans of the nations; he thwarts the purposes of the peoples. But the plans of the LORD stand firm forever, the purposes of his heart through all generations (Ps. 33:10–11).

The LORD Almighty has sworn, "Surely, as I have planned, so it will be, and as I have purposed, so it will stand." . . . For the

LORD Almighty has purposed, and who can thwart him? (Isa. 14:24, 27).

My purpose will stand, and I will do all that I please. . . . What I have said, that will I bring about; what I have planned, that will I do (Isa. 46:10–11).

God is the world's greatest Planner. He has planned all His creation. God is the world's great Coordinator, who makes all things work together for our good and for His purpose. "And we know that in all things God works for the good of those who love him, who have been called according to His purpose" (Rom. 8:28).

Joseph's brothers tried to eliminate him from their lives to keep him from the success God was promising him. They were totally unsuccessful. Others can hinder you for the time being and seek to harm you. But no one can ultimately hurt you. If God permits temporary suffering, He will abundantly reward you—usually in this life, but always in eternity. His guidance will lead you to His success.

4. *God's guidance envisages the end from the beginning.* God knows not only the eventual result of His plan for you, but also your loss if you follow your own plan.

I make known the end from the beginning, from ancient times, what is still to come. I say: My purpose will stand, and I will do all that I please (Isa. 46:10).

In him we were also chosen, having been predestined according to the plan of him who works out everything in conformity with the purpose of his will (Eph. 1:11).

Since God knows the possible end result of any action even before it is done (1 Sam. 23:9–13), He is able to give perfect guidance at any moment in the light of any potential situation. He is able to choose for you what you would choose if you could see and know perfectly as He does.

5. *God's guidance assures His infinite power to accomplish His purpose.* God is the Sovereign of the whole universe. Heaven's wisdom, resources, and angels are at His disposal. God is for you when you are doing His will and fulfilling His plan. "If God is for us, who can be against us?" (Rom. 8:31). The Psalmist voiced it

well: "The LORD is with me; I will not be afraid. What can man do to me? The LORD is with me; he is my helper" (Ps. 118:6–7). Isaiah said to God's enemies, "Devise your strategy, but it will be thwarted; propose your plan, but it will not stand, for God is with us" (Isa. 8:10). Satan cannot touch or stop us without God's permission. The all-important question is, are we guided by God? Are we in the center of His will?

God is eternally sovereign over all. He is able to coordinate what is best for you with what is best for others and for His total plan. God's will for you is *shalom* (complete fulfillment, wholeness, unimpaired relations with others, and fulfillment of your undertakings). God does not sit on the sidelines, observing your pain saying, "Oh well, it will be good for you in the long run." Never! God's will is not usually disagreeable. His will becomes the joy of those who are surrendered and Spirit-filled. Do not dread or fear it. When His Word, His law, is in your heart, you—like the psalmist—will come to desire and delight in God's wonderful will (Ps. 40:8).

God is a Shepherd who constantly has your welfare on His heart. He is your loving Father who was willing to give His only Son for you. True, like a skilled surgeon, He must sometimes permit painful procedures, but it is only to make you whole and happy. It is only what you yourself would choose if you knew as He knows. He plans to give you a great future (Jer. 29:11). He is the Divine Planner you need. He is the One whose guidance you must seek and follow. None other can take His place.

4

god plans to guide you

God is a God who plans. Even before the world came into existence, God had a great, overarching plan for time and eternity. That plan included His plan for creation, for redemption, and for the eternal ages. You were chosen in Him to be holy even before the creation of the world (Eph. 1:4). Within His great, overarching plan of the ages, God had planned for Israel's worship and gave the plan to Moses (Exod. 26:30). God seems to have shown him in a vision a model of the tabernacle. Later David testified that God gave him the complete and detailed plan for the temple.

> He gave him the plans of all that the Spirit had put in his mind for the courts of the temple of the LORD. . . . "All this," David said, "I have in writing from the hand of the LORD upon me, and he gave me understanding in all the details of the plan" (1 Chron. 28:12, 19).

Is it surprising, then, that God not only plans for the course of history but also for your life and mine? Because of your ability to obey or disobey, God makes constant adjustments of the details of His plan for you. But God's sovereign power guarantees that His overall plan will be fulfilled. You can miss part of God's plan for you or disqualify for participation in His plan (Heb. 10:36; 2 John 8; Rev. 3:11). But God will carry out His basic, divine purpose. And He always stands ready to incorporate you into His plan to the extent that you obey Him. Isaiah assures us, "This is the plan determined for the whole world" (14:26).

"I know the plans I have for you," declares the LORD, "plans to prosper you and not to harm you, plans to give you hope and a future" (Jer. 29:11).

Because God Plans, He Guides

Among the many promises of God's guidance given in the Bible, several are very precious:

The LORD will guide you always (Isa. 58:11). He never takes His eye or His hand from the life of His obedient child.

"I am the LORD your God, who teaches you what is best for you, who directs you in the way you should go" (Isa. 48:17).

I will instruct you and teach you in the way you should go; I will counsel you and watch over you (Ps. 32:8, NIV).

Lean not on your own understanding; in all your ways acknowledge him, and he will direct your plans (Prov. 3:5–6, alternate trans.).

Whether you turn to the right or to the left, your ears will hear a voice behind you, saying, "This is the way; walk in it" (Isa. 30:21).

Besides offering detailed promises of guidance, both the Old and New Testaments provide many examples. Christian biography adds thrilling details of what God wants us to experience.

The God who constantly plans gives full attention to all within His plan—all people and all details. Look at the amazing mathematical detail in the composition of the atoms throughout the whole universe, whether in the stars or in the molecules of your body. It is all essential to His plan of creation.

The God who planned for the church and sent His Son to be our Savior plans for every need of the church. He not only guided in the inspiration of Scripture, but continues to be available to guide in the translation, publication, and distribution of Scripture.

The God who inspired David to write the Psalms guided and anointed Henry F. Lyte so strongly as he wrote "Abide With Me" that it was almost as if God dictated it. He so guided and anointed

Handel in the writing of his great oratorio *Messiah* that Handel seemed to see heaven opened and God seated on His throne. God guided as much in the writing of the music as the words of the "Hallelujah Chorus." Which is more spiritual—the words, or the music? Foolish question! They belong together.

Quoting John 16:13—"The Spirit of truth . . . will guide you"—Abraham Lincoln added, "I have so many evidences of God's direction that I cannot doubt this power comes from above. I am satisfied that when the Almighty wants me to do, or not to do, any particular thing, He finds a way of letting me know it."

Your life's plan is a part of God's plan of the ages. You and God's plan belong together. You are personally loved by God. Even your hair is of interest to Him. It may not be important enough to you to number, but God has the number. Jesus said so (Matt. 10:30). Samuel Chadwick wrote,

> The humblest followers of Jesus may know the Divine will at firsthand. "It is every man's privilege to be fully assured in the will of God." The Divine attention to detail is amazing. Nothing is too trivial for omniscience.[1]

Guidance begins even before you are converted, as God's goodness and love seek to lead you to repentance (Rom. 2:4). When you are born again and become God's child, guidance enters into a new and wonderful dimension. Now the Holy Spirit lives in you as your divine Counselor. When you totally consecrate yourself to God and ask Him to fill you completely, you are even more available to Him and open to His guidance. Your yieldedness makes you more sensitive to His gentle voice and touch.

Guidance Now and in Eternity

Guidance is your eternal privilege. "This God is our God for ever and ever; he will be our guide even to the end" (Ps. 48:14). "You guide me with your counsel, and afterward you will take me into glory" (Ps. 73:24). He will guide you through death into heaven's glory, and into the fullness of heaven's realization.

Life in eternity will be greater than you have ever conceived

---

[1] A. Skevington Wood, *Life by the Spirit* (Grand Rapids: Zondervan, 1964), p. 64.

of—more wonderful, more meaningful, and more beautiful. Forever and ever He who is now your Shepherd will continue His guiding role. You will no longer need His protection; but His guidance will be your need and joy throughout the fulfillments of eternity. "For the Lamb at the center of the throne will be their shepherd; he will lead them to springs of living water. And God will wipe away every tear from their eyes" (Rev. 7:17).

By promise, example, and instruction, the Bible pictures divine guidance as God's plan for your life. God does not want you to see His guidance as something exceptional that may happen a few times in the lifetime of some special saints. He plans to guide you daily. Often you will be conscious of it, but often you may not be aware of it until later.

J. H. Gilmore caught this theme of Scripture as he wrote:

> He leadeth me, O blessed thought!
> O words with heavenly comfort fraught!
> Whate'er I do, where'er I be,
> Still 'tis God's hand that leadeth me.
>
> He leadeth me, He leadeth me,
> By His own hand He leadeth me!
> His faithful follower I would be,
> For by His hand He leadeth me.

You can live a normal yet supernatural life. God adds a dimension to lift you above the common and ordinary. The supernatural dimensions He adds include salvation, the fullness of the Spirit, prayer, and guidance. Can you testify with Paul, "Thanks be to God, who always leads us in triumphal procession in Christ" (2 Cor. 2:14)? You too can be God-directed daily.

Like all other aspects of your Christian life, a God-directed life is both privilege and duty. It is easy to experience if you learn to live and walk in the Spirit; it is impossible unless you do. If you are unsurrendered, unyielded, or insisting on your own desires and way in things, guidance will be sporadic at best. Once you taste the joy of the guided life, you will not want to revert to a life that forgets this privilege in Christ.

Once while I was in Britain for speaking engagements, I arrived at Lebanon Bible College a bit earlier than I was expected, and my room was not ready. I went to a seat on the lawn and began a blessed time of prayer with the Lord. Suddenly a student arrived, obviously sent to entertain me. For a moment I was tempted to resent this interruption in my communion with the Lord. Then I thought, "Maybe God sent him."

The student asked if I would not like to see the river Tweed, which flows just below the college. As we walked, I said, "Isn't it wonderful that God is so concerned about us and has a plan for our lives!" I began to describe the joy of knowing God's will. Suddenly he stopped and looked at me. "You don't know what you are doing," he said. "For months I have been trying to find God's will for my life." What a blessed time we had together as I helped him to see God's availability to guide us. Later when I got to my room, I wrote this poem. It was October 24, 1958.

Jesus Has a Plan for You

What a privilege God gives
To the one who for Him lives.
God, the great omniscient One,
Gladly owns him as His son.
He prepares a perfect plan
For each consecrated man.

If we choose His perfect will
He each promise will fulfill.
He will make as clear as day
All our steps along His way.
Though the future He conceal,
Step by step He will reveal.

He who walks through life with God
Will not blindly grope and plod.
Jesus holds by His right hand
Those obeying each command.
He's responsible for you
When His perfect will you do.

Oh, the joy of guidance clear!
Oh, the peace when He is near!
How triumphantly you go
When each step you guidance know!

Faith keeps changing into sight
When you seek and walk in light.

Jesus has a plan for you;
Trust Him for that plan anew.
Praise Him, love Him, just believe
And His guidance you'll receive.
Step by step He'll clear the way;
Praise Him, trust Him, and obey.

avoid extremes in guidance

One extreme in guidance is to forget that clear guidance is the privilege of every child of God and one of God's evidences that we are born again. "Those who are led by the Spirit of God are sons of God" (Rom. 8:14). They interpret this verse as referring mainly to our growth in grace. They forget the comprehensive promises of Scripture and the many biblical examples of guidance in very practical matters.

If you have never learned the joy of a guided life, you are missing one of the great blessings provided by God's grace. You are missing the precious deepening of assurance that comes every time guidance is prayed for and received. You are in danger of remaining fairly unacquainted with much of the ministry of the Holy Spirit. You miss many opportunities of being used by God and miss the joy that always comes when you are conscious of being thus used.

Some Bible teachers go so far as to teach that God's will for us contains few details. God's plan for our lives is mainly concerned with our salvation, and perhaps at times our life's vocation. In many other situations we can please God equally whatever we decide. They believe God is glad to bless whatever we choose to do; it makes little or no difference to Him.

They may say, "Oh, that is too small a detail. Don't bother God about that! Just use your common sense and do what you want to do." Of them it may be said, as in the verse of the hymn,

O what peace we often forfeit,
O what needless pain we bear,
All because we do not carry
Everything to God in prayer!

One may almost wonder if they have a very close friendship or communion with Jesus. Do they not share the details of their lives with God in prayer? Or do they pray and expect God to listen to them but never to speak in return? That would be a very one-sided conversation!

Avoid Expecting a Special Word About Everything

There is another extreme: expecting special guidance in everything. In many situations you need no additional divine guidance. They are covered by the clear teaching of God's Word or by principles based on God's Word. Other situations are covered by having "the mind of Christ" (which will be discussed later).

When you are following a path into which God guided you, continue in that path until He gives you new instructions. Do not keep questioning your past guidance. God is responsible to alert you when He has new instructions.

Many of the details of daily living need not be questioned unless the Lord specially alerts you or restrains you. Commit yourself to the Lord's guidance each day and then live normally. But live in the expectation that God may at any time have some new, special touch or gentle suggestion for you.

Avoid Flaunting Your Guidance

When God guides, you rarely need to announce that "God told you." Some people almost make themselves obnoxious by constantly telling others, "God told me to do this" or "God said this." It is usually far better to follow humbly in the path of God's guidance without announcing it. Let God put His seal on your obedience by His providence.

God may give very personal messages for you to tell someone. Be sure that God is guiding you, and then go ahead. God sent Nathan to David with an important message for him (2 Sam. 7:5).

My mother went through four years of serious physical need— pneumonia, pleurisy, a heart condition, partial paralysis, and other complications. Several times she seemed near death's door. Eventually cancer developed. One day God instantly healed, and she lived many years longer.

But once during her illness, Mother went through a period of great depression when Satan accused her that God no longer loved her. Because of her weakened condition, she was unable to throw off these accusations. She wept by the hour. One day God sent an evangelist, who knew nothing about the depression, many miles to give Mother a brief message: "God sent me to tell you He loves you." Then the evangelist left. God used that simple but direct message to begin Mother's complete recovery from the depression.

But some people erroneously count every impression, or almost any thought that comes to them, as the voice of God. An independent missionary lady announced that God told her a certain minister and wife were to go to the mission field under her private mission board. The minister replied, "God hasn't told me yet." Over the succeeding years, he and his wife often thanked God that they did not accept this good lady's "guidance."

A missionary was "led by God" to buy a rocky hillside for an orphanage. The land proved totally undesirable and for years was almost impossible to resell. But she had proclaimed to everyone that God had led her to this property!

Others almost every week announce details of what God "told" them. Most of these things are comparatively innocuous, but often a bad taste is left in others' mouths, and the testimony of the person tends to be weakened by such frequent claims.

Some people become so impressionistic that they do odd and unwise things. They may get in such bondage to their impressions that they start one activity or ministry and then feel impressed to change, until they leave many projects incomplete and make fools of themselves. They may even become psychologically disturbed. This is totally unnecessary.

God does guide, and He guides very clearly. He does often give very strong impressions as one aspect of His guidance, but these can be properly checked and validated to verify that they are from God, as we will see later.

all of your life
is sacred to god

The Spirit's loving guidance is available for all the details that are important to daily living—your health, your everyday work, your travel, your relations with others; in fact, your whole life.

God does not divide your life into two divisions with all that you consider religious or sacred in one category and all that you consider more secular or of little concern to Him in another. It is not possible to make a sharp dichotomy between the spiritual and the practical steps and details in guidance and life.

God created you to be a whole person relating to all of life. He desires to make all your life sacred by His presence, guidance, and blessing. The Holy Spirit is given to guide and bless every aspect of your living. Seemingly spiritual things can be done in very secular and unspiritual ways. Seemingly normal, unspiritual things can be done in ways that are blessed and guided by God. An act that is secular in itself can reflect God's presence, goodness, and glory when He guides you.

To be guided in manifesting spiritual love is spiritual, but that may involve guidance in many mundane details and practical steps. You cannot separate spiritual love from any part of life. Guidance in witnessing is spiritual, but may involve guidance as to which store you enter, or which checkout clerk you go to, or which restaurant you eat in, or which highway you take to buy your gasoline.

I heard Charles E. Gremmel, a businessman, tell how he was

speeding from Boston to an appointment when he suddenly felt the Spirit's impression to stop at a filling station he was passing. He braked the car and swung back into the lot and up to the gas pump. "My," said the attendant, "you must have really needed gas!"

Gremmel asked him, "What oil do you sell?" The attendant listed several brands.

"Do you have the Oil of Joy?" asked Gremmel.

"Never heard of that," replied the attendant.

"That's strange," said Gremmel. "My Father manufactures it."

Then Gremmel began to witness. He found the man was mourning the death of a wife who for years had prayed for him. That day a new name was written in heaven because Gremmel had a "listening ear" while driving his car.

When Philip won the Ethiopian eunuch to Christ, God's guidance included the timing of his trip and the exact road to take. God even sent an angel to guide in these details, which in themselves did not seem "spiritual." God does not play games with you by dividing your life into some compartments which He is interested in and others where He keeps hands off.

God Is Interested in Everything

God does not say, "I am concerned about your sin, but not about your pain." He is interested and available to guide in your friendships, your daily work, the scheduling of your time, your reading habits, and the use of your money. I have proved that He is equally willing to guide you in discovering just the book you need to read or just the bargain you need to buy.

George Washington Carver, renowned black scientist, invited God to go with him into his research laboratory every morning. God did, and He guided him there. God delights to guide a mechanic in locating problems in making repairs or a secretary in locating important information. Whatever your situation, God loves you and will gladly guide you. You can learn to commit yourself, trust, and then receive guidance.

To be guided is a blessed but sometimes awesome experience that never grows old. Let me give examples of this from my personal experience. There is joy in being guided in spiritual ministry. Once while I was in the British Isles I ministered on a

Sunday morning and evening in a Baptist church on the south coast of England. After the last service, several came individually to say how God had guided in the messages. One said, "Oh, if you knew, if you only knew our church, you would know how those messages were exactly what we needed."

It is equally a joy to be guided in such mundane things as making purchases. I had prayed for weeks about whether to buy a certain new type of camera. I wanted to get only the kind of camera God would have me get. I visited at least seven camera stores in the city in which I resided, but none stocked this particular camera.

I passed through another city en route to a speaking engagement and felt led to stop there. I knew I had not more than an hour to spend if I were to reach my evening appointment on time. I drove to the center of the city and spent about twenty minutes trying in vain to find a parking spot near a phone booth. Finally I prayed, "Lord, if You want me to get the camera, show me a parking spot and guide me to the right store."

When I saw a vacant parking place, I went into a small store, asked to see a phone book, and turned to the Yellow Pages. At the list of camera stores, I prayed, chose one, and, putting my finger on the name, asked the clerk where this store was located. "Just around the corner!" he said to my amazement.

I entered the camera store, approached the manager, and asked if he had a used camera of the model I wished. "Yes," he replied, "I have used this one myself, but I am willing to sell it to you." Instantly I prayed, "Lord, don't let me make a mistake."

Just then another customer entered the store. The manager said to him, "Hi, Reverend."

I looked at him in surprise. "I'm a missionary," I confessed.

The minister told me, "Well, I'm the one who gets almost all the camera supplies for such and such a mission. I get most of them here." He leaned over to me and added quietly, "You can trust this man; his word is as good as gold. I have been trying to witness to him. I know God has been talking to him."

I began to testify how God had saved me and how I wanted to share with everyone what Christ meant to me. Something I said prompted the minister to chime in, "You know, I used to be in show business, and I played in the _____ theater here."

"You did!" said the manager. "Why did you give that up?"

Then the minister gave his testimony. The manager seemed almost excited as he said, "Isn't that something, that you two should meet each other here!"

I added, "Yes, and that you have the very camera I need." The manager seemed almost overawed.

"Let's pray," we said. The Jewish store manager bowed his head as we prayed with him. I paid for the camera—a price that I could afford—and hurried to my car. As I climbed in, I glanced at my watch. All this had happened in about a half hour! I drove on my way rejoicing at how precisely God had guided, giving the affirmation of a Christian minister and an opportunity to witness. How good God is! And I made it to my appointment on time.

Living in guidance does not make you irresponsible, nervous, and impressionistic. It lets you live in the relaxed joy of knowing that God is constantly looking out for you, thinking ahead for you, making arrangements for you. He delights to be your Friend, your constant Companion, and your constant Guide.

7

Guidance in things large and small

Guidance is the universal need of man. No one knows enough about the past, present, or future to constantly make correct decisions independent of all counsel from others or from God. God planned to be man's Helper above all other helpers, man's Counselor above all other counselors.

Jeremiah confessed, "I know, O LORD, that a man's life is not his own; it is not for man to direct his steps" (10:23). Solomon wisely admitted, "A man's steps are directed by the LORD. How then can anyone understand his own way?" (Prov. 20:24). He also stated, "Many are the plans in a man's heart, but it is the LORD's purpose that prevails" (Prov. 19:21; see also 16:9).

We need God's guidance in the great decisions and events of life. We equally need guidance in details, the seeming minutiae. How often what seems a tiny detail has major consequences!

You Need Guidance in Major Decisions

Everyone has to make major decisions: marriage, purchase of a home, farm, going into business for oneself, attending college or seminary, Christian service, moving to another state or city, retirement. Some decisions that seem major at the time turn out to be fairly unimportant. Others that seem comparatively minor turn out to have tremendous implications for your life.

One Sunday afternoon while I was at a missionary vacation

center in India, God led me to walk back into the mountains along a specific road instead of attending the evening church service. As I walked along praying, I met a missionary friend.

Out of this "chance" meeting on the mountain road God provided a much-needed faculty member who gave years of effective missionary service as part of the OMS family.

Moses asked God's guidance for a successor to him, and God pointed out Joshua. God told Elijah to anoint Elisha to be his successor. God guided in the anointing of Saul, David, and Jehu. God also guided Paul to go to Jerusalem and eventually to Rome.

You Need Guidance Even in Small Details

No detail is too small for God's interest and His counsel. Nothing important to you is trivial to Him. The most ordinary action can lead to far-reaching and eternal results. Jacob sent Joseph on a walk to check on the welfare of his brothers, but it led to his being sold into slavery, becoming prime minister of Egypt, and being the cause of Israel's sojourn and survival in Egypt.

God was tremendously concerned with the details when He chose Saul to be the first king of Israel. Samuel told Saul that when he reached Rachel's tomb he would meet two men who would tell him about his father's donkeys. Then when he got to the large tree at Tabor, he would meet three men. One would be carrying three small goats, one three loaves of bread, and one a skin of wine. The man carrying the bread would give him two of the three loaves. When he reached the slope to the high place at Gibeah, he would meet a procession of prophets coming toward him, and they would be playing lyres, tambourines, flutes, and harps. Then the Holy Spirit would come on Saul and make him a new person.

The Bible says all these signs were fulfilled (1 Sam. 10:9). God was trying to teach Saul how minutely He knew all the details of Saul's life, how able He was to control the actions of people, and how important it was for Saul to obey in little things.

On one occasion, after retreating to safety from the Philistines, David asked the Lord if he should attack them (2 Sam. 5:19). God told David to go and attack them; David did and won a great victory. The Philistines attacked again, and David asked if he shoul engage them in battle again. He did not take it for granted that just because God gave him one victory He would give another.

God then gave minute battle descriptions: David was to outflank the enemy and then wait until he heard the sound of marching troops in the leaves of the balsam trees. This sound of God's troops joining the battle was the sign for David to attack. David won a decisive and far-reaching victory, demonstrating that every detail of God's guidance was important.

Jesus taught His disciples to be guided in small details. When He sent two of His followers to prepare for the last supper, He told them to go to the gate of Jerusalem and there they would see a man carrying a jar of water. When God guides, He coordinates all details and prepares all who are involved in the situation.

The sacred and the secular cannot be separated. Just as God put the Book of Proverbs between the books of Psalms and Isaiah, so God makes apparently trivial incidents or actions opportunities for spiritual results. Just as in Proverbs there are moral precepts interspersed between precepts for practical daily living, so God interweaves the practical and the spiritual in all of life.

Apparently small incidents can by the Spirit's guidance provide special opportunities for God's will to be done. "Be very careful, then, how you live—not as unwise but as wise, making the most of every opportunity. . . . Understand what the Lord's will is" (Eph. 5:15–17). What does Paul mean by "opportunity"? It includes the opportunities to live for God and be used for spiritual blessing to others along with the opportunities for being a good neighbor, a helpful friend, and a good citizen.

It could be that who you sit beside decides whether or not you find a person like Lydia (Acts 16:14), whose heart has been prepared by the Lord. Normally it will not make much difference. But if you live a life committed to guidance and practice listening for the Spirit's leading, He will gladly guide you and the other person whom you need to sit beside.

One Sunday morning just as Mrs. J. Sidlow Baxter entered her usual pew at church, she suddenly felt strongly impressed to change and sit in a seat near the front beside a woman who was going through deep family problems. She hesitated for a moment, but felt a peaceful assurance that she was being guided by the Spirit.

Nine months later the woman she sat by told Mrs. Baxter that on that Sunday she had been so embarrassed by her family problem that she considered avoiding the scandal by dropping out of the church. That morning she prayed, "Dear Lord, guide me. Preserve me from unwise inquirers, and if it please Thee, may Mrs. Baxter come and sit with me." Mrs. Baxter had a listening ear to the prompting of the Spirit, and the woman's need was met.

Several years ago as I mounted the steps of a plane in a western state, I breathed a prayer, "Lord, if there is someone You want me to sit beside, please arrange it." Seats were not preselected, so I went and sat in an empty row. Shortly afterward a Roman Catholic priest came in and sat beside me. I immediately asked the Lord to guide me if there was any special way I could be a blessing to him.

As the plane took off, I began to read my Bible. After a while I turned to the priest and said, "There is a tremendous responsibility upon us in Christian ministry these days, isn't there?"

He replied, "There certainly is." I shared my testimony.

The priest turned to me. "You know, I believe the Lord wanted me to sit beside you today!"

I replied, "I'm sure He did," and told what I had prayed.

He said, "I am on a very difficult trip. The head of my Order is seriously ill with a brain tumor. I am en route to try to be an encouragement to him. Will you pray for me?"

I prayed for him. As we stepped into the aisle to disembark, the priest said, "Now you are going to pray for me, aren't you?" I replied that I would. As we started down the plane steps, he turned to me again and repeated, "You will pray for me, won't you?" Again I assured him I would. Just as we entered the building he was paged, and I discovered he was the bishop of Montana.

We need guidance more often in the small details of our lives than we do in the major decisions. But the Holy Spirit is interested in everything. He is the Lord of providence. He is the Lord of the practical. Nothing is too small for Him to be involved in.

8

you can learn
to be guided

God's gracious provisions for us are so simple that new Christians and even children who are walking with the Lord begin to experience them almost without realizing it. Take prayer as an example. You begin to pray as soon as you are saved and almost without realizing it learn more and more as you go on. You learn from the study of the Bible and from the examples of other Christians. Even children require little teaching to begin to pray. Then, as they grow older, learning to pray can become a wonderful, lifelong experience.

In the same way, every child of God begins to be led by the Spirit in simple, natural ways. New Christians begin to be guided in their spiritual lives, in daily details, and in times of special decision. Clear scriptural teaching and the examples of godly Christians can teach them much more and can help growth in guidance to be far more rapid and blessed.

Do you have a hunger to be led more constantly and more clearly? That desire is God's gift to you. The Holy Spirit has been given to you to be your Teacher and Guide and to fulfill your desire.

1. The Holy Spirit desires to lead you into a guided life. "He will guide you into all truth" (John 16:13). God's will for you is part of the truth into which He is sent to guide you. The Holy Spirit is more desirous of leading you than you are of being led.

2. The Holy Spirit often leads you when you are not aware. He is your Guide whether you have asked Him to guide you in a specific situation or not. You may forget; He will not. Often you may look back and realize with joy that He guided you better than you understood. When you recognize this, be sure to thank Him.

3. *The more the Spirit guides you, the easier it will become to recognize His guiding voice or touch.* As you discern His hand on your life, He builds up your faith and trust and you begin to await expectantly the next indication of His leading you. You will become more aware that it is He who is speaking to you, touching your life, or gently holding you back from some unwise action. Gradually His guiding hand becomes your spiritual habit.

4. *Ask God each day for His guidance.* Ask Him to guide you each day in your prayer life. He may do this by impressing you to pray more fully for one of the names or items on your prayer list. You can ask Him to give you someone specially to pray for each day, and then pray for that one at free moments throughout the day. You may be led to pray for a person or situation that was not even on your mind. Trust Him to guide you each day in your prayer.

Ask God to make you a special blessing to someone each day. Ask Him whom you can bless that day with a "for Jesus' sake" smile, a "for Jesus' sake" helping hand, a word of encouragement, a gospel tract, or some other way. Ask God to guide your witness.

One New Year's during my college days I asked God to make me a blessing to someone each day that year. At times, if I had found no one, I would walk out on the street asking the Lord to guide me.

As I left the college grounds one sunny afternoon, I prayed, "Lord, where is the person I should bless today?" I turned toward a residential area and soon saw a drunken man staggering along the sidewalk. Never before or since did I see a drunk in that area. Putting my hand on his shoulder, I said, "Brother, God loves you." Instantly he threw both hands up in the air and called aloud, "Oh, God, be merciful to me, a sinner! Be merciful to me, a backslider!" I gave him a gospel tract, told him God could change his life once more, and when he left me he walked down the street praying. I knew he was God's assignment for me that day.

It was almost midnight of a cold winter's day, and I had not consciously been a blessing to anyone. I hurriedly put on my overcoat, took a few gospel tracts in my hand, and started out. The snow was falling. Not a person was in sight. I walked to the corner. "Lord, where is the person I am to bless today?" I felt I should turn left. I walked a long block, praying. Still no one was in sight, and the snow kept falling. "Lord, where is the person I should reach?" I prayed. I felt impressed to cross the street. No sooner had I done so than a streetcar rounded the corner two blocks away. I stood praying. The streetcar stopped right in front of me, and a man got out and stepped onto the sidewalk right where I was standing. My heart leaped for joy. Here was the man I was to bless! I handed him the gospel tract and returned to the college.

On a Sunday morning another student and I returned to the section of the city where we were doing gospel visitation. We were ready to begin at the next house, but for some reason one of us asked, "Does God have some other plan today?" Praying, we walked on, turned to the left, walked two blocks, turned right. Ahead was a large apartment building. We felt impressed to go to the top, to the sixth floor. A few steps led up to a low door.

A woman came to the door. We explained that we were visiting homes to read the Bible and pray with people. She said, "Follow me." We came to a room with an invalid man in bed. We started to explain our visit. Immediately the man spoke up, "For six months I have been praying that God would send someone to pray with me." In this poverty-stricken home we were in God's place at the right time. The hearts were ready, and the people were soon in tears as we prayed with them.

5. *Ask God repeatedly to guide you in any assignment He has for you.* I was visiting a seminary in India and entered the seminary chapel for the last service of their Deeper Life Convention. As I sat beside a student, an inner voice seemed to say to me, "You did not ask where to sit." I do not normally ask where to sit. "No, Lord," I said. "Where should I sit?" I felt impressed to go to the front of the chapel and to the left.

When I got to the front I saw one student sitting alone on the left. I went over and sat beside him. Instantly he looked at me with an anxious face. "I need so much to know God's will," he said to me. I replied, "Let's go outside and pray together."

God had completely prepared his heart. We found a secluded

place and prayed together. I knew God had sent me to counsel and help him. There was a strong sense of God's Spirit surrounding us. I knew that was at least part of the reason God had arranged for me to be at that seminary that day.

While on furlough from India I gave the message one afternoon at the missionary service in a large convention. That night I was part of the platform party. After the anointed message by an evangelist, I bowed my head and prayed for people to respond. As they began to sing the invitation hymn, I asked the Lord, "Is there anyone here whom I am responsible to reach tonight?" I had not done this before. My eye was drawn to a man far back in the large auditorium on the left side.

Praying, I slipped off the platform and went back to that man. No one else was going back to speak to people, but I felt impressed to do so. Before I completed my first sentence as I began to say, "Would you like to go forward to pray tonight?" the man started forward. I was almost stunned by his instant response. Standing there in the aisle, I bowed my head: "Lord, is there anyone else?" I saw a person about ten feet away to whom I felt drawn. I went there and, again, almost instantly he also went forward to pray. In the next two or three minutes I spoke to five persons, and each one went forward to make a commitment to Christ. Then I felt a sense of release from my responsibility. I felt almost shocked by what had happened in those moments, as I prayed, "Lord, what if I had not asked You?"

In regard to guidance, as in other spiritual matters, undoubtedly so often, "You do not have, because you do not ask God" (James 4:2). How often have you and I been missing opportunities because we failed to ask God for His assignments?

6. *Trust God to suggest to you simple things for you to do for Him.* As you ask God for things to do, you will begin to find that guidance becomes more and more frequent, in fact, an almost natural part of your daily experience. Then when you need Him in special major moments of decision, guidance will come more easily.

you can Be GuiDeD continuously

Since the Holy Spirit is given to counsel, since He is named your "Counselor," and since you need His counsel repeatedly, you have every right to expect His counseling ministry to be one of the most consistent experiences of your spiritual life.

When God led Israel out of Egypt, He did not just supply the visible pillar of cloud and fire when there was some crisis, when enemies were near, or when they were to begin a new stage of their journey. The cloud and fire were the constant, visible manifestation of God's presence with them day and night. In the Old Testament, when Israel kept close to God, His guidance was His normal provision for their daily living.

Jesus experienced daily guidance during His earthly life. He is our pattern in continuous guidance. Many Bible teachers agree that Isaiah 50:4 refers to Christ, the Servant of the Lord: "The Sovereign LORD has given me an instructed tongue, to know the word that sustains the weary. He wakens me morning by morning, wakens my ear to listen like one being taught."

Jesus showed perfect dependence on God's guidance. He was always teachable. He was guided in His words: "I did not speak of my own accord, but the Father . . . commanded me what to say and how to say it. . . . So whatever I say is just what the Father has told me to say" (John 12:49–50; cf. Isa. 50:4; John 7:16; 14:10, 24). Jesus was equally guided in His deeds (John 5:19, 30; 8:28).

When Isaiah declares, . . . "The LORD will guide you always" (Isa. 58:11), he is reiterating one of the basic undertakings of Scripture. "The idea of steadfast providential guidance," according to T. G. Selby, "is one of the fixed polar ideas of both the Old and New Testament." . . . The believer . . . can no more doubt the guidance of God than he can doubt his own existence.[1]

Led by God's Hand

The Hebrew verb used in Isaiah 58:11 in the expression "guide you always" is *naha*. It means to conduct one along the right path. Note another use of the same word: "I am always with you; you hold me by my right hand. You guide me [*naha*] with your counsel, and afterward you will take me into glory" (Ps. 73:23–24).

Your guide, the Holy Spirit, is always with you. He holds you by His right hand, leads you along the right path, and speaks words of counsel to you until He leads you into heaven's glory. How beautiful! Constant presence, constant holding of your hand, constant counseling and leading for you! Your Good Shepherd leads you until you are "in the house of the LORD forever" (Ps. 23:6).

Andrew Murray writes, "The lower steps of the ladder are low enough for the weakest to reach; God means every child of His to be led by the Spirit every day."[2]

God wants your guidance to be as continuous as your spiritual growth. Jesus is with you whether you realize it or not; He observes you and protects you whether you realize it or not. Even so, He can guide you both when you realize it and when you are not even aware of it. Guidance can be blessedly your daily experience.

God's guidance is typified by the sun. God is our Light. "The LORD God is a sun and shield" (Ps. 84:11). The clouds can hide the sun, but it is still there. You may go long periods without the benefit of conscious guidance; but God is always there, guiding you far more carefully and constantly than you realize.

Guidance is to be as continuous and as certain as sonship.

---

[1] A. Skevington Wood, *Life by the Spirit* (Grand Rapids: Zondervan, 1964), p. 62.

[2] Andrew Murray, *God's Will: Our Dwelling Place* (Springdale, Pa.: Whitaker House, 1982), p. 129. (Formerly titled *Thy Will Be Done*.)

Guidance should be inseparable from sonship. "Those who are led by the Spirit of God are sons of God" (Rom. 8:14). God's loving interest in you includes not only your spiritual welfare, but also all else that is important to you, even the little details of your life.

Guidance in Your Spiritual Life and Growth

God's loving guidance includes all that relates to your walk with the Lord. Whatever is essential to your spiritual growth is important to God and to you. It is wonderful to be a newborn Christian, a new babe in Christ. But God does not want you to remain a spiritual infant. Spiritual growth can be far more rapid than physical growth. In many Christians, however, spiritual growth is tragically slow.

Paul expressed concern about this: "Brothers, I could not address you as spiritual but as worldly—mere infants in Christ. I gave you milk, not solid food, for you were not yet ready for it. Indeed, you are still not ready" (1 Cor. 3:1–2). "Brothers, stop thinking like children. In regard to evil be infants, but in your thinking be adults" (1 Cor. 14:20). The writer to the Hebrews urges, "Let us leave the elementary teachings about Christ and go on to maturity" (Heb. 6:1).

One of the main roles of the Holy Spirit is to guide believers to spiritual maturity. He wants to mature the fruit of the Spirit in you (Gal. 5:22–23). How does this occur? By living in the Spirit and keeping "in step with the Spirit" (v. 25).

The Spirit desires to guide you in your prayer and intercession—a major aspect of the Christian life. Often you do not know in yourself what you ought to pray for, or when someone at a time of crisis needs your prayers (Rom. 8:26). The Spirit helps you in your weakness and guides your prayer.

He desires to guide you in your Bible reading, meditation on the Word, and careful study. " 'No eye has seen, no ear has heard, no mind has conceived what God has prepared for those who love him'—but God has revealed it to us by his Spirit" (1 Cor. 2:9–10). We have "the Spirit who is from God, that we may understand what God has freely given us" (1 Cor. 2:12). God has spiritual blessings for you, spiritual treasures hidden in His Word. He wants you to feed on them, to grow by them, and to revel in them.

The Spirit desires to guide you in your witnessing to others, in your showing loving goodwill to others, and in your service to others. He wants to bless the world through you. He desires to make you ever more Christlike and more effective in living for Christ and serving Christ. He, your Counselor, will lead you in all these important spiritual ways.

Resident to Guide You

Your Counselor indwells you all the time. He is resident to guide you in all your activities. Since that is His special role to you, He desires to interweave His guidance with all parts of your living. Each day He wants to make His guidance natural and normal. He is not there to dominate you or take over your personhood. He is there to make you effective as a person. He desires to bring His suggestions to your mind—whether positive or negative—in such a natural, normal way that you hardly realize it.

You will not normally sense a strong guiding urge or restraint. When you are living a constantly guided life, the absence of strong guidance may be just as satisfying as God's strong touch on your life. But you may experience this kind of clear guidance at any time.

10

GOD'S WILL AND GOD'S PERMISSION

God's will and God's guidance are two beautiful, spiritual realities. They are closely related and complementary. They are God's gracious provision for you, and it is important that you understand both. They are often so closely associated in the Bible and in experience that at times we use "guidance" and "the will of God" to mean almost the same thing. But there are important distinctions between the concepts. First, let us look closely at the will of God.

The Bible speaks often of God's will. All that God has ever done has been according to His will. He created first the angels and all heavenly beings, then the universe and earth (Job 38:4–7), and finally man. He chose man to be created in His image, capable of choice and capable of holy fellowship with Him. Since choice involved the possibility of sin, His provisional plan provided for the incarnation and death of Christ (Rev. 13:8). Thus the whole plan of salvation and its outworking were part of God's gracious plan for the ages and were all part of God's holy will.

In one sense, God's will is one unitary whole.[1] Because of this, we can pray either comprehensively or, in a specific situation, the prayer Jesus taught us, "Your will be done" (Matt. 6:10). In another sense, God's will consists of many details.

---

[1] Colin Brown, ed., *The New International Dictionary of New Testament Theology.* 4 vols. (Grand Rapids: Zondervan, 1975–1986), III:1022.

God is the great First Cause of all, but by His wisdom and will the laws of nature and even human beings can become secondary causes. We call God's ordained, regular way of working "laws of nature" or of science or of health. But remember, God is not a slave to His laws. He is always free to work out His holy purpose by temporarily transcending any law of nature. We call this "miracle," but to God it is merely His work. He does nòt break or change His law; rather, He sovereignly transcends it for the moment.

Two Aspects of God's Sovereign Will

The "will" of God is not always a fixed decree. It is often used in the Bible in the sense of God's plan, purpose, or desire. By far the most common word in the Greek New Testament for God's will is *thelēma*. It is used for that which God wills or emotionally desires. It comes from the verb *thelō,* which "usually expresses desire or design."[2] (Note Rom. 1:10; 2 Cor. 8:5; Eph. 1:5, 9, 11; and Heb. 10:36.)

God wills all people to come to repentance (2 Peter 3:9) and be saved (1 Tim. 2:4). But not all do. F. F. Bruce comments on Ephesians 1:11, "His will may be disobeyed, but his ultimate purpose cannot be frustrated, for he overrules the disobedience of his creatures in such a way as to subserve his purpose."[3]

We are responsible to understand the Lord's will (Eph. 5:17). It is "foolish" (Gk. *aphron,* "to lack common sense, to be without reason") not to do so. Paul prayed constantly for his converts to be filled with the knowledge of God's will (Col. 1:9). W. E. Vine comments, "The will of God, as mentioned here, does not mean the counsels of God regarding salvation, nor His counsels as made known to us in Christ, but His will for the conduct of our lives, so that we may 'walk worthily' of Him."[4]

Epaphras prayed that the Colossians would "stand firm in all

---

[2] W. E. Vine, *An Expository Dictionary of New Testament Words* (London: Oliphants, 1940), pp. 1228–29.

[3] F. F. Bruce, *The Epistles to the Colossians, to Philemon, and to the Ephesians* in *The New International Commentary on the New Testament* (Grand Rapids: Wm. B. Eerdmans, 1984), pp. 263–64.

[4] W. E. Vine, *The Epistles to the Philippians and Colossians* (London: Oliphants, 1955), p. 201.

the will of God, mature and fully assured" (Col. 4:12). On this Vine comments, "Here the meaning is not the will of God as a whole, but in every detail of it."[5]

Let us look at God's sovereign will in two ways. Andrew Murray divides God's sovereign will into the will of approval and the will of permission.

1. God's will of approval. This includes all that God does by His plan, choice, and volition. He does it because He wills it. He is the responsible cause. This is always the wisest and the best. This includes all that God does in creation, preservation, and redemption. It includes the outworking of salvation and all in the universe that is holy, righteous, just, moral, and essentially good. All that you need to know of God's will of approval is revealed in the Bible—in its statements, examples, and the principles derived from its truth. You live in the center of God's will as you live according to Christ, His teaching, and all that is revealed in Scripture. And this will of approval is general; it is the same for you as it is for all.

In any decision or action on which there is Bible teaching, you have there the clear, authoritative will of God for you. You need not ask questions, pray about it, or seek guidance in additional ways. Scripture settles it. You may need to pray, study God's Word, and receive the counsel and teaching of a mature Christian to help you understand better some particular point; but the Bible is the ultimate authority for your life. When you know what it teaches, you know God's will and guidance for you in that matter.

2. God's will of permission. All that happens in our world is obviously by God's permission. If He does not intervene to prevent it, He has permitted it. But this does not make God the responsible cause of all that happens. It is a slander on God to say that He causes accidents, inflicts suffering, and sends war. He does not normally intervene to transcend secondary causes or to restrain them. He can do so. He can forgive, answer prayer, guide, restrain, or perform a miracle. Miracles are extraordinary acts of God, not His normal acts. God is the responsible cause of creation and redemption, but most things that occur in our lives are through secondary causes. Note these categories:

---

[5] Ibid.

a. *Nature and its laws are secondary causes*. God is the author of nature and its laws. Through nature's law we receive benefits and blessings. We also may receive harm: lightning, flood, earthquake, typhoon, fire, rain, drought, health, pain, illness are all related to nature and its working. The more science advances, the more we learn how to regulate, control, and use the laws of nature for good. It is because of man's sin that the human race is so slow to learn these things.

b. *Human beings are secondary causes*. God created man with the power to be a secondary cause. Because you are part of the human scene you greatly benefit from the wise use of abilities, resources, time, and the power of choice by others. What would you do without government, roads, education, medicine, invention, organization, and many other things of which man is the responsible cause? God permits persons to use personhood in wise, responsible, and beneficial ways.

   But because you are part of the human scene you may also suffer loss, problems, pain, and even death by the way others unwisely use their abilities, resources, time, and power of choice. A car may be used helpfully or for a crime. Chemicals can be used for medicine or for illegal drugs. Again, man is the responsible cause.

   If a building collapses with loss of life, don't say that God willed the death of these people. If the building was not constructed properly, man is the responsible cause. True, God created the law of gravity, and He created man with the ability to learn how to build. The people died by God's permission, because He did not intervene to put extra bracing in the building by miracle power. And He does not normally do that.

c. *Satan can be a secondary cause*. God created Satan a holy being with power to be a secondary cause. Satan sinned and became the enemy of God and man. He deceives people, incites them, and uses them if they will obey him. Occasionally, as with Job, God temporarily permits Satan or his demons to manipulate aspects of nature. But this is only within the limits of action and time God sets. God is still sovereign. He does not normally restrain Satan from tempting. Until the time foretold in the Book of Revelation (20:2), Satan is permitted to be a secondary cause in some ways.

Normally God permits His laws of cause and effect, sowing and reaping, choice and result to continue without interference. We can use them for good or evil. He has created us so we can learn from the experience of others. But if we are too unwise, careless, or stubborn to learn from the experience of others, we will have to learn many things the hard way, on our own.

God did not intend death. He warned Adam and Eve that sin destroys and kills. Sin brought death into the world as its consequence (Rom. 5:12). It is unjust to say that God wills the death of a person by drugs, alcohol, or terrorism. He permits it in the sense that He does not interfere with a person's misuse of his brain, emotions, or choices. He does not kill a person because he begins a destructive habit or cultivates hatred and cruelty. It is a slander on God to say He wills sin, suffering, or destruction.

Listen to God's voice: "Repent! Turn away from all your offenses; then sin will not be your downfall. . . . For I take no pleasure in the death of anyone, declares the Sovereign LORD. Repent and live!" (Ezek. 18:30–32). Millions perish every year spiritually through their sin and physically through secondary causes. But God is a God of love, goodness, and blessing. God is "not wanting anyone to perish" (2 Peter 3:9).

To summarize, God loves you infinitely and personally. He has given you a personality with Godlike powers. Around you are adequate resources to benefit you and others. But you must choose constantly. You were created to choose. God does not normally intervene and transcend secondary causes—that is, your free will, the law of gravity, the conflagration, sowing and reaping. He is always available to you, to forgive and help in spite of sin and mistakes. He is available to guide you, to answer prayer, and to help you in time of need.

So if you have received Christ as your Savior and are seeking to please God, to do His will, and to live wisely, your primary concern is not with God's sovereign will, but with aspects of His personal will for you, and especially with His good guidance for you.

what the will of god means for you

Just as from God's perspective there are two aspects of His sovereign will—His will of approval and His will of permission—so from the perspective of man's responsibility God's will includes two spheres—revealed direction and graciously permitted choice.

God's Directive Will (You obey)		God's Will Permitting Choice (You need guidance)
The plan of salvation; Christian standards of action	1	The unfolding of life's choices
General—the same for all believers	2	Individual—according to each one's need
Usually has moral implications	3	May or may not have moral implications
Essential to please God	4	Essential to most effective living and service
Revealed in Scripture	5	Revealed by personalized guidance
Unchanging	6	Flexible, adapted to life's changes and opportunities
Revealed once for all	7	Revealed step by step
God's gracious provision	8	God's leading and help to appropriate His provision
Your highest priority	9	Your next-highest priority

Evidenced by the witness of the Spirit and a holy life

The supreme responsibility of the Spirit: to transform you as you obey

Your responsibility: to believe, ask, receive, obey, and remain steadfast

Role of Spirit: to point you to the Word and fulfill the Word in you

10 Evidenced by inner peace, providence, joy, God's blessing

11 The supreme responsibility of the Spirit: to guide, anoint, help, give wisdom, give results

12 Your responsibility: to listen, ask, use wisdom

13 Role of Spirit: to lead you
- in all matters involved in effective Christian living, prayer, witness, and blessing to others
- in practical details involved in wholesome decisions; effectiveness in vocation; usefulness in family, church, and community; smooth interpersonal relations; and wholesome daily living

1. God's revealed direction. God's approved will for you is already revealed in His Word. You accept it as God's personal word to you, for it was written for you. God does not compel your acceptance. He created you to choose, and you must make God's will your own by obedience. By accepting it, you become related to God's great eternal plan and fulfill His purpose for you.

God's direction for you is the same for all. It includes repentance; new birth; being cleansed, filled, and empowered by the Holy Spirit; growth in grace into ever-increasing holy likeness to Christ; the fruit of the Spirit; holy living; and a life of intercession, witnessing, and blessing others. Ultimately it includes glorification and sharing in heaven. God's revealed direction incorporates you into God's eternal plan for His church and for eternity.

There is no option for you if you want to please God in everything. God's will is revealed. It is your authority. You may neglect or disobey, but you do so at your own loss.

2. *God's will permitting choice.* The other sphere included in God's will is His gracious provision of continual choice. The Holy Spirit has been given to you as your Counselor to guide you in your choices. If you are totally committed to God's will; if you keep close to the heart of God; if you keep a listening ear and observant eyes, sensitive to the indications of the Spirit's guidance and restraints; if you keep open and obedient—you can live wisely and effectively.

The Holy Spirit is responsible to alert you or keep you from serious mistakes, to coordinate providence so as to make your obedience possible, and to assist you in all essential needs. He coordinates your living in accordance with God's ongoing plan.

The highest priority of the Spirit is to point you to the Savior and His full provision for spiritual needs; to apply the fullness of salvation; to make and keep you victorious in holy living; and to guide you in every way necessary to make this possible.

The second-level priority of the Spirit is to be your Companion-Counselor in all the mundaneness of living. No one is more practical than the Holy Spirit. No one is more constantly with you to help you. No one is more eager to be a part of all your living. When He fills you He is constantly available to guide you, enable you, and anoint you. Much of the time you are almost unconscious of His presence, guiding, and enabling. "I am the Lord your God, who teaches you what is best for you, who directs you in the way you should go" (Isa. 48:17).

It is when you depend on yourself more than on Him, when you are self-confident rather than trusting, when you are so absorbed in your own efforts rather than appropriating His wisdom that you have your problems. They are permitted to drive you back to Him, to awaken you out of your self-sufficiency to total dependence on Him. They are intended to lead you away from lapses of self-seeking (1 Cor. 10:24; 13:5) and into living above all else for God's glory (Col. 3:7; 1 Peter 4:11).

Grace Is for Practical Living

No one who understands the heartbeat of Scripture can apply its principles only to "spiritual" matters. Of course these have priority, but righteousness and holiness are meant for living. Grace is as available for you in the practical details of life as it is for the worship of God. Guidance begins in the realm of salvation, but extends to all of life. Indeed, your most constant need of guidance is in your daily routines and choices, so that all you do—even your eating and drinking—is done to the glory of God (1 Cor. 10:31).

Wise Solomon wrote, "In all your ways acknowledge him, and he will direct your paths" (Prov. 3:6 marg.). "All your ways"—not just the large decisions, but all decisions; not just in spiritual matters, but in all matters. The Hebrew word translated "acknowledge" is really a very strong and intimate word: *yada*. It means "to have the closest fellowship with; intimate acquaintance." God "knew" (*yada*) Moses "face to face" (Exod. 33:17; Deut. 34:10). He knew (*yada*) when David sat and when he rose, and He knew (again *yada*) all his thoughts (Ps. 139:2). When we constantly in all our ways keep intimately close to Him and know Him in the most intimate communion, we increasingly *know* His guidance.

Does this truth make you neurotic, indecisive, and erratic in decision making? To the contrary, it leads you to joyful commitment, restful trust in God's faithfulness, and joyful awareness of His involvement in all your living. It makes prayer, trusting, listening for His guidance, leaning on His power, and loving obedience almost as natural as breathing. It makes us want to sing:

> The Comforter has come, the Comforter has come!
> The Holy Ghost from heaven, the Father's promise giv'n;
> O spread the tidings 'round wherever man is found—
> The Comforter has come!

The fullest meaning of the Greek word *paraklētos* entails the concepts of "counselor, helper, one called to one's side to aid." So we could substitute words and also sing that chorus, "The Counselor has come!" or "The God Who helps has come!" or "The Anointing One has come!" All praise to our Lord!

12

the blessedness of god's will

Nothing is more blessed than to know that you are in the will of God. And you can know. If there was anything Paul was sure of, it was the will of God. This assurance "dominated his whole ministry—inspiring at once devotion, obedience, and perfect confidence."[1] He recognized that God's purpose was being worked out in his life. In five of his letters he asserts that he is an apostle "by the will of God" (for example, 1 Cor. 1:1).

Paul's trip to Rome was "by God's will" (Rom. 1:10; 15:32). Paul was so sure he was in God's will that he let no event, no threats of danger, no plots of his enemies, and no tears from his friends turn him back. He had experienced God's guidance for years, and he was sure he was in God's will now. It was one of the most far-reaching decisions of his life. He pressed on (Acts 20:22–24; 21:10–14). The result was that God's church spread in Rome, and the epistles of Ephesians, Philippians, Colossians, 1 and 2 Timothy, Titus, and Philemon were written.

Paul writes poignantly: "Be very careful, then, how you live—not as unwise but as wise, making the most of every opportunity. . . . Therefore do not be foolish, but understand what the Lord's will is" (Eph. 5:15–17). The word Paul gives for "under-

---

[1] Andrew Murray, *God's Will: Our Dwelling Place* (Springdale, Pa.: Whitaker House, 1982), p. 83. (Formerly titled *Thy Will Be Done*.)

stand" is not the one he normally uses. This one means "to bring together." In understanding the will of God in major decisions, we bring together the insights from God's Word, our personal sense of God's leading or restraining, the various related providential circumstances, and at times the counsel of others.

In the practical, routine affairs of life we bring together our duties, our opportunities, our skills, and our sense of God's direction and blessing thus far. We continue in the general path that He has blessed up to this point and until He gives us a new sense of direction or an inner uneasiness or a sense of being possibly held back from what we might have done.

We will discuss each of these factors in the chapters that follow. Thank God, we can have a satisfying knowledge of God's will. Paul told the Colossians, "We have not stopped praying for you and asking God to fill you with the knowledge of his will" (Col. 1:9).

Life Is Choices

The will of God has to do with life, opportunities, and choices. Do not be "foolish" (the Greek word means "lack of common sense in the perception of the reality of things"). Make the most of each opportunity by a wise choice, because God's will is something to be understood and lived out each day.

As life unfolds, God permits you to make new choices. In each one, as you depend on God's conscious or unconscious guidance, you continue to live out the will of God. Because your life is constantly related to God and is lived in the light of eternity, your life and God's eternal plan become one whole. You do not discover that plan once for all like a celestial blueprint with every detail outlined in advance. No, you expect—and by faith accept—God's guidance day by day in all your activities and choices. God's will becomes for you, in the words of Andrew Murray, "one whole— equally Divine, beautiful, and blessed."[2]

Since you know you have committed yourself unreservedly to God as a living sacrifice (Rom. 12:1–2), you expect to receive His guiding touch continually and you seek to make all choices in ways that are wise and pleasing to Him. Each day He equips you with

---

[2] Ibid., p. 104.

whatever you need to do His will (Heb. 13:20–21): insight, wisdom, courage, guidance, strength, and His anointing on your life. So you have the blessed assurance that you are living all of life in the will of God. You are a living example of the prayer Jesus taught you to pray, "Your will be done on earth" (Matt. 6:10).

Lloyd John Ogilvie says, "God is in search of us! He wants to communicate His ultimate will and His daily guidance."[3] As you live in the will of God, following His purpose and guidance, you find you know God better and better. As we walk in the light we receive more light; the light is brighter and shines farther (Prov. 4:18). As we move forward in the path already clear, God shows the next steps ahead.

Paul had this thought in mind when he wrote to the Christian slaves in Ephesus to do "the will of God from your heart" (Eph. 6:6). God's word to you and me is clear: we too can do the will of God in everything. We can live our lives as unto the Lord whether we brush our teeth, comb our hair, polish our shoes, or work at a desk or in the kitchen. Because we are totally surrendered to do His will, we have the assurance that all of life is beautiful to God, fragrant for God, and in the will of God.

God's Will Is Blessed

God's will is so blessed! There need be no fear, no strain, no worry. Rejoice in God's love and goodness. Rejoice in His faithfulness to alert you, guide you, or restrain you in the commonalities of life. Doing His will from your heart means that you love Him, desire to please Him, delight in His goodness, expect His help and blessing, and expect Him to guide your thinking, decisions, and choices. You expect Him to touch your life constantly. You make every moment of your living a joyful love-gift to Jesus. You are in Christ, abiding in Christ, living in guidance.

This becomes almost automatic. "Whatever you do, whether in word or deed, do it all in the name of the Lord Jesus, giving thanks" (Col. 3:17). "Whatever you do, work at it with all your heart, as

---

[3] Lloyd John Ogilvie, *Discovering God's Will in Your Life* (Eugene, Oreg.: Harvest House, 1982), pp. 9–10.

working for the Lord, not for men, since you know that you will receive . . . a reward" (vv. 23–24).

Let us notice these briefly now:

1. Blessed because of strength. God's will is blessed because you are strengthened as you do it. Jesus said, "My food . . . is to do the will of him who sent me and to finish his work" (John 4:34). Just as food strengthens, satisfies, and gives joy and well-being to the body, so discovering and doing the will of God gives inner strength, satisfaction, and joy to the spirit. It is spiritually nourishing to do the will of God. It gives a strong sense of spiritual well-being.[4]

Eating is the way you appropriate food. Doing God's will is the way you appropriate new guidance and the will of God. God reveals the next step to the one who obeys and acts on the guidance he already has. "Then you will be able to test and approve what God's will is—his good, pleasing and perfect will" (Rom. 12:2). The Greek for "test and approve" implies a process of testing like gold repeatedly tested during its purifying in the furnace.

2. Blessed because of peace. God's will brings deep inner peace. It gives you a blessed assurance that God is with you. God's promises come alive. You rest more deeply and assuredly on His faithfulness. You know He will not let you make a serious mistake without guiding or cautioning you (Isa. 30:21).

3. Blessed because of joy. God's will is blessed because it brings so much joy. As you delight yourself in the Lord (Ps. 37:4), your will and God's become as one. There is no greater satisfaction than knowing you are in God's will. Nothing thrills you more than to realize God has been guiding you even when you did not realize it. What joy to see God fit providences together in His perfect timing! It is so beautiful to see evidence that He has been planning for you.

4. Blessed because of fellowship with Jesus. God's will draws you so close to Jesus. Seeking and doing the will of God increases communion. "Whoever does the will of my Father in heaven is my brother and sister and mother," Jesus said (Matt. 12:50). The more you live in God's will, the more you prove your love for Jesus and the more He responds with outpourings of His love, His joy, and

---

[4]M. Blaine Smith, *Knowing God's Will* (Downers Grove, Ill.: InterVarsity Press, 1979), p. 39.

His goodness. The more you seek to please the Lord in everything, the more joy Jesus finds in you. Guidance makes you Jesus' companion.

5. *Blessed because of the unbroken presence of Jesus.* It is in communion that you find the power both to discern and to do the will of God. I am not speaking merely of special mountaintop spiritual experiences. Rather, I refer to daily, almost hourly, communion as you commit your way to the Lord and thank Him for His promise of guidance and for the way He keeps guiding you.

The two strands will become blessedly interwoven: the more you keep praying, praising, and loving Christ without ceasing, the more you will find yourself expecting and receiving little hints of guidance on the practical affairs of your day. You go from communing moments to communing moments, and from His guiding hints to other guiding hints. And as you bring communion and guidance more and more into your life, you will find more and more the awareness of His constant nearness.

No parent ever watched his child with such interest and love as your heavenly Father does every detail of your life. No older brother ever watched over a younger brother with such identifying concern as Jesus, your elder Brother, has for you. No husband ever watched his bride with such affectionate devotion, longing to guide and help, as Jesus watches over you. How blessed that as you long with ever more yearning for the fullness of the will of God in all your living, so you are bonded ever more closely to Jesus!

This does not imply that living constantly in God's will in the details of your life involves no disappointment, problems, or unanswered questions. Involvement in the human scene cannot avoid these. But living in God's will, living in the Spirit's guidance, adds a sacredness to all of life. It is blessed!

13

GOÒ IS A GOÒ WHO SPEAKS

God is a God who speaks. From all eternity the three persons of the blessed Trinity—God the Father, God the Son, and God the Holy Spirit—have been speaking, fellowshiping, and communing with each other. When God created angels He created them to speak and communicate. They share in the fellowship of heaven by speaking in praise and worship. Then God created man to speak.

God has spoken to us in the past through prophets, but now speaks through His Son (Heb. 1:1–2). The period of Christ's incarnation was preeminently a period of His speaking. Throughout His earthly ministry Jesus was constantly speaking to individuals and groups—speaking the very words of God (John 7:17; 8:26, 28; 12:49–50; 14:10).

The Holy Spirit is today, above all, our speaking God. Today the Trinity speaks to us primarily through the Holy Spirit. Jesus assured us that the Holy Spirit listens to the Father and the Son and speaks "only what he hears" (John 16:13). He takes what Jesus shares with Him and makes it known to us (v. 14), and Jesus says that is what is actually given to Him by the Father (v. 15).

The Trinity is a speaking Trinity, with much to say to us in (1) teaching, (2) guidance, and (3) fellowship. One main contrast between Jehovah and the false gods of the pagans is that Jehovah speaks. He always has something to say and He says it.

Often when God has something to say He lacks someone to

listen. God had something to say during the two hundred-plus years of the judges before the time of Samuel. But Scripture says, "In those days the word of the LORD was rare; there were not many visions" (1 Sam. 3:1). After the time of Joshua, God spoke to Gideon (Judg. 6:11–23), when the Ammonites attacked (10:11–14), and to Samson's parents before his birth (13:3–21).

Had God nothing more to say? Indeed. Were there no true believers in those centuries? Certainly, but none who sought God until they heard His voice. God may at times test you by His silence in order to increase your faith. But God is a God who loves to fellowship with you, to listen to you, and to speak to you. You were created to communicate and fellowship with God.

God Also Listens

God is also a God who listens. He "heard" Abel's blood calling to Him. So we can say that God hears what He sees and sees what He hears. In other words, He gives full attention to all we say and do. He knows our need before we ask Him. God heard the child Ishmael cry (Gen. 21:17). Rachel testified that God listened to her (Gen. 30:6). God listened to Leah (Gen. 30:17). He listened to Israel when they prayed (Num. 21:3), when they grumbled (Deut. 1:34), and when they talked to Moses (Deut. 5:28).

God listens when we speak together of Him and keeps a record so He can one day reward us (Mal. 3:16–18). We do not even need to speak audibly for God to hear us. He sees and hears the cry of our hearts, the hidden longing that we may never reveal. He heard Hannah when she prayed silently (1 Sam. 1:13, 27).

The Bible Is Filled With History of God's Guidance

God obviously gave guidance to Adam's family, or Cain and Abel would not have known what kind of sacrifice was acceptable.

Enoch's walk with God involved communion and guidance. God spoke to Noah and guided in many details concerning the ark. God called and led Abraham; He spoke through Christ's preincarnate form as "the angel of the Lord." Abraham's servant testified that God led him (Gen. 24:27). Isaac, Jacob, Joseph—all were spoken to by God or led by God.

God guided Moses in the most minute details of steps he was

to take and the sacrifices and ceremonies he was to institute, and He confirmed this by repeated visible evidences of His approval.

The Lord sent the pillar of cloud and fire to lead Israel. No group of people has ever been so visibly, continually, and supernaturally led of God. Surely God was trying to teach mankind that all His people can be led by Him.

God arranged for continuing guidance after the death of Moses by providing the Urim and the Thummim (Exod. 28:29–30). At times God permitted people to use the casting of lots to discern His will. These were especially used by people unaccustomed to the voice of God. God spoke directly to the judges and prophets to give them guidance for Israel and her kings.

David may have been the only king to whom God spoke repeatedly and directly. In 1 Chronicles 28:19 David describes God's detailed guidance in words similar to Ezekiel's: "the hand of the LORD" was on him.

The Bible Contains Beautiful Testimonies of Guidance

Abraham's servant confessed, "As for me, the LORD has led me on the journey" (Gen. 24:27). David testified, "He leads me. . . . He guides me" (Ps. 23:2–3). Asaph said, "You guide me with your counsel" (Ps. 73:24). Paul rejoiced, "Thanks be to God, who always leads us" (2 Cor. 2:14).

In the early church God gave clear guidance through the direct voice of the Holy Spirit, visions, or angels to Philip, Ananias, Cornelius, Peter, and Paul.

Christian biography also testifies to God's unfailing guidance when we meet His conditions. George Mueller said,

> I never remember in all my Christian course, a period now 69 years and four months, that I ever sincerely and patiently sought to know the will of God by the teaching of the Holy Spirit, through the instrumentality of the Word of God, but I have always been directed rightly. But if honesty of heart and uprightness before God were lacking, or if I did not patiently wait upon God for instruction, or if I preferred the counsel of my fellowmen to the declarations of the Word of the living God, I made great mistakes.

14

you cannot afford to miss god's plan

You and others also may miss great blessing if you miss the major intent of God's plan for your life. To fail to hear God's guiding voice, to fail to respond to God's restraint, or to be oblivious of God's plan can be far more significant than it first appears to be.

If you neglect your health, you may develop great physical problems. If you neglect your mind and and do not discipline your study habits, you may lose much educationally and, as a result, lose the potential of your life and work. But if you neglect to find God's will or to discern His guidance, you risk great loss in every aspect of your life and much of your eternal reward.

David's Mistake

David was a man repeatedly guided by God. He normally sought God's will in everything. But on several occasions he failed to get divine guidance, and each time there was loss. For many reasons he thought it was God's will to bring the ark of the covenant to Jerusalem. David thought that bringing the ark to the center of the nation would draw them all nearer to God. But he failed to ask God how he should do it; then Uzzah was smitten by God and the nation's rejoicing suddenly turned to sorrow. It was three months before the ark was finally brought. David learned his lesson and later explained his mistake: "We did not inquire of him about how to do it" (1 Chron. 15:13).

David was one of the greatest administrators in Bible history. As a young man he took a totally unorganized nation and did a job of administration comparable to what Moses did in the wilderness. David organized the temple worship, the Levites, the singers, the priests, the tribes, and the army. He made lists of the names of all these in the process. But when he numbered the fighting men, he failed to get God's guidance and was probably partly influenced by pride. God sent a punishing pestilence on the nation, and 70,000 died (1 Chron. 21). David had missed God's will in one detail, and the whole nation suffered.

Jehoshaphat's Mistake

Jehoshaphat was one of the greatest and godliest kings of Judah. God was with him (2 Chron. 17:3); he sought God (v. 4) and was devoted to God's ways (v. 6). God used him to bring revival to the nation. Jehoshaphat sent teaching priests to bring the people back to God. Later he himself went out and helped bring renewal to the nation. On one occasion he said, "First seek the counsel of the LORD" (2 Chron. 18:4). God gave him a tremendous military victory through simply praising the Lord.

Yet on one occasion Jehoshaphat failed to get God's guidance. Solomon had built a fleet, sent it to Ophir, and received seventeen tons of gold (2 Chron. 8:18). Jehoshaphat decided to do the same, building his fleet at the same seaport. But God sent a storm and wrecked the ships before they sailed. Jehoshaphat had failed to ask the Lord's guidance.

Hezekiah's Mistake

Hezekiah was one of the greatest and godliest kings. He too was used by God to bring great revival to the nation. Devoted to God from his youth, on the first day of his reign he began to turn the nation back to God. God healed him in answer to his prayer. The whole history of Hezekiah's rule until the very end is one of God's blessing.

Then Babylon sent emissaries to congratulate Hezekiah on his recovery, and he failed to get God's guidance as to how to entertain them. Hezekiah made a great mistake, and this probably put the first desire into the heart of Babylon's rulers to conquer Judah.

Eventually Babylon took Israel into captivity. If only Hezekiah had sought and obtained God's guidance in that detail!

Josiah's Mistake

The holiest person can become careless and assume he knows what God's will is and make a great mistake. David, Jehoshaphat, and Hezekiah did. Josiah was another king much used by God. He was the last great hope of the nation. He was God's instrument in bringing the last revival to Judah. He interceded for the nation, weeping before God. What a man of God!

Yet Josiah failed to get God's guidance when the king of Egypt passed nearby. Josiah was killed at an early age, and within twenty-five years the nation went into captivity. If only this godly king had sought God's guidance in this one matter! Had he lived longer, Josiah might have led the revival deeper until the whole nation was changed. But he missed God's plan.

Jeremiah's Mistake

Jeremiah was the great "weeping prophet" of Israel. How mightily God used him to minister to the nation even though they often failed to listen to God's voice through him! Many times God used Jeremiah to give individuals or groups God's will. When Jerusalem was finally captured by Babylon as Jeremiah had prophesied, he was given the choice to stay in Jerusalem or go with the other captives.

But Jeremiah failed to make a choice, apparently having no guidance. So Nebuzaradan made the choice for him and told him to stay. Within months, Jeremiah was forcibly taken to Egypt, prophesied a short time, and was never heard from again. Perhaps if he had sought God's guidance, he would have chosen to go with the captives and been able to carry on a great ministry among them. Did Jeremiah miss the will of the Lord?

Keep close to God so you can quickly sense His guidance or restraint. Keep a listening ear daily to all God may have to say to you. Follow the steps to God's guidance as delineated later in this volume. Don't miss God's plan! Don't miss some of the reward and crown that God wants to be yours (Rev. 3:11).

15

commitment is essential in guidance

To find guidance in any situation, you must commit it wholly to the Lord. This means to take a completely neutral attitude, a "not my will but yours" attitude. And then to actively put the responsibility in His hands.

An uncommitted situation leaves you with a bias. This bias may be unconscious, but it can easily mislead nevertheless. You are not truly "open" to God in any situation you have not fully committed to Him. Martin Wells Knapp wrote, "Any mental reservation in the commitment will deaden the discerning of the divine voice."[1] And James Jauncy said, "The Lord will not cross the picket line of the will. . . . Throughout the Bible . . . in almost every case it seems the person called was willing to do God's will before it was ever revealed."[2]

Spurgeon testified, "Brethren, I can testify for my God that when I have submitted my will to His directing Spirit, I have always had reason to thank Him for His wise counsel. But when I have asked at His hands, having already made up my own mind, I have had my own way; but like as He fed the Israelites with quails from

---

[1] Martin Wells Knapp, *Impressions* (Cincinnati: Revivalist Publishing House, 1892), p. 85.

[2] M. Blaine Smith, *Knowing God's Will* (Downers Grove, Ill.: InterVarsity Press, 1979), p. 38.

heaven, while the meat was yet in their mouth, the wrath of God came upon them."[3]

Augustine prayed, "Grant that we may never seek to bend the straight to the crooked—that is, Thy will to ours—but that we may bend the crooked to the straight—that is, our will to Thine."[4]

Make a Total Commitment

But there is a deeper level of commitment. To make guidance your normal experience, your holy lifestyle, total commitment must become the state of your soul. "Commit your way to the LORD" (Ps. 37:5). This is more than a specific situation. It is the commitment of your whole life, your whole being, your whole way.

> Therefore, I urge you, brothers, in view of God's mercy, to offer your bodies as living sacrifices, holy and pleasing to God—this is your spiritual [alternate translation: 'reasonable'] act of worship. Do not conform any longer to the pattern of this world, but be transformed by the renewing of your mind. Then you will be able to test and approve what God's will is—his good, pleasing and perfect will (Rom. 12:1–2).

Your "body" here represents your whole being, your whole life. In the Old Testament the sacrifice was to be slain. Paul urges you to offer yourself as one spiritually alive. You offer to live fully in accordance with the will of God and to let Him do whatever He will. You place your total self, your total future in His hands. You make your life, as it were, a blank check that you sign and hand to God to fill in all the future details as He desires at any time and in any way.

This commitment of self is done in advance. You turn over the authority to God regardless of how He chooses the future. It is a faith commitment. It is also a final commitment. The tense of the Greek verb translated "offer" indicates a decisive, once-for-all step that is so final it brings a decisive result.

---

[3] Knapp, *Impressions,* pp. 85–86.

[4] Quoted in Lloyd John Ogilvie, *Discovering God's Will in Your Life* (Eugene, Oreg.: Harvest House, 1982), pp. 155–56.

What Your Commitment Means

Commitment means your will is so decisively presurrendered that from then on you can truthfully say that the whole set of your soul, your whole daily life, demonstrates the words of Christ, "I seek not to please myself but him who sent me" (John 5:30). It is a constant living sacrifice of your will.

Your self-commitment is to be "holy [made pure by the Holy Spirit] and pleasing to God." (*Logiken* can be translated either "spiritual" or "reasonable.") This, says Paul, is your spiritual and reasonable way of serving God. He wants you as His priest to offer yourself. This is the most spiritual act you can perform in worship of God, and in view of God's great mercy to you it is the most reasonable step you can take as a Christian.

So what does this mean in your life? Paul answers in the subsequent words. It means you "do not conform any longer to the pattern of this world." The world is self-seeking, self-promoting, self-centered, self-willed. But when you make this once-and-forever total commitment you become Christ-seeking, Christ-promoting, Christ-centered, Christ-willed.

You will then be able to testify with Paul, "I [my carnal self-will] have been crucified with Christ and I no longer live, but Christ lives in me" (Gal. 2:20). How can this become factual in you? By the Holy Spirit. The Spirit cannot cleanse, empower, and fill you until you are utterly empty of your carnal self-will, having nailed it to Christ's cross. Then the Spirit can take full control. What does He do after that? He transforms you by "the renewing of your mind," your nature, the whole attitude of your being. The Greek word translated "mind" means the inner man, the ego, the real self.[5]

When you have been thus renewed, you begin such liberty, such Spirit-enabled living, that, as Paul says, "You will be able to test and approve what God's will is—his good, pleasing and perfect will." Daily you experience the joy of the fullness of His will. Daily you test and prove, decision by decision, how faithfully God keeps you in His will.

---

[5] Colin Brown, ed., *The New International Dictionary of New Testament Theology*. 4 vols. (Grand Rapids: Zondervan, 1975–1986), II:127.

Andrew Murray explains it, "After our regeneration, the secret, subtle atmosphere with which the world surrounds us, and with which the flesh is in alliance, hinders thousands of Christians from seeking a life of true and full devotion to the will of God."[6]

Paul's constant prayer for the Colossians was for God "to fill you with the knowledge of his will through all spiritual wisdom and understanding" (Col. 1:9). To be filled means your whole being is pervaded and penetrated with the knowledge and experience of God's will—your thoughts, attitudes, desires, and plans. But you cannot be thus filled until you have emptied yourself of self-will.

Don't consider God's will a long list of dos and don'ts. It is "God's grand will—the controlling power of the life, inspiring and animating the whole being."[7] If you have not made this "absolute surrender," make it today.

Total Commitment Prepares for the Spirit's Infilling

Absolute surrender is the necessary foundation for the guided life, but it is also much more. It is the essential preparation to being filled and keeping filled with the fullness of God the Holy Spirit. Oh, that all of God's children would live constantly in the Spirit's fullness! The promise of Jesus was that His followers would be filled (Luke 24:48; Acts 1:8 with Acts 2:4, 39). Full consecration is the very blessed but negative aspect of the even more blessed and positive glory of being filled with the Spirit.

The Holy Spirit can cleanse us from all that impedes Christlikeness, spiritual growth, and effective living only when we make that absolute surrender. Then we can ask and receive all the fullness of the Spirit's indwelling. The fruit of the Spirit, Spirit-energized praying, and the guidance of the Spirit are the outflow, the normal result of His infilling.

This was the secret of power that transformed Charles G. Finney and catapulted him into powerful revival ministry. This was the secret that transformed D. L. Moody when, after years of busy and zealous working for Christ, he had this crisis experience and

---

[6] Andrew Murray, *God's Will: Our Dwelling Place* (Springdale, Pa.: Whitaker House, 1982), p. 80. (Formerly titled *Thy Will Be Done*.)

[7] Ibid., p. 111.

became a worldwide influence for God. It is the spiritual secret of thousands of lesser-known but graciously used Christian workers, and it is the secret of holy living for millions of God's children marked by godly lives and outpoured, Christlike love. It can be your secret of Christlikeness, prayer power, and guidance.

Ask and you will receive. "If you then, though you are evil, know how to give good gifts to your children, how much more will your Father in heaven give the Holy Spirit to those who ask him!" (Luke 11:13). Make the total commitment today. Then ask today for the Spirit's mighty infilling. You, like the apostles in Acts 4:31, can have repeated infillings of the Spirit. Has your spiritual life seemed dry and empty? Ask to be refilled today.

The Spirit's fullness results in His extensive working in and through your whole being and life. The pervasiveness of the Spirit's work within you leads to His new gracious control of your life in a new completeness. It brings a new dimension of the Spirit's direction and enabling. George D. Watson comments,

> To him who is crucified to self the Holy Spirit grants an illumination and direction incomprehensible to imperfect believers. He can discern in the providence of the Father a special significance and minuteness which others are blind to. He can detect clear indications of God's will in the written Word which others grossly stumble over, and besides these he can hear that inner voice of the Spirit, can know the touches of a divine finger on his soul impelling him along his God-given orbit.[8]

The Spirit transforms you in order that you may discern and prove God's perfect and pleasing will in your daily living (Rom. 12:2). The Spirit illumines and applies God's Word, developing within you the mind of Christ. The Word applied by the Spirit trains you to distinguish good and evil in your daily living (Heb. 5:14). It is the interrelated ministry of the Spirit and the Word that guides you. The Spirit reminds of, illuminates, and applies the Word. The Word substantiates, clarifies, and prevents misinterpretation of the Spirit's voice.

The Holy Spirit gives you that finer quality of discrimination, not merely between what is good and what is evil, but also between

---

[8] Knapp, *Impressions,* p. 92.

what is good and what is better or best. "So that you may be able to discern what is best" (Phil. 1:10). The Spirit shows you not only "the most excellent way" of love as compared with emphasis on gifts (1 Cor. 12:31), but the most excellent way in practical living—in interpersonal relationships, speech, and witness for Christ.

> He leads by inspiring us with a life and disposition out of which right principles and decisions come forth. . . . He that would have the leading of the Spirit must yield himself to have his life wholly possessed and filled by the Spirit. It was when Christ had been baptized with the Spirit that he, "full of the Spirit . . . was led of the Spirit in the desert."[9]

Levels of the Spirit's Guidance

There are three levels or ways the Spirit leads us. A first level is His bringing to your attention things you would otherwise have overlooked. Usually you don't even realize that the Spirit has guided your thoughts. Because He fills you, He directs your thoughts from within without calling attention to His help. This is the more common and normal method the Spirit uses.

A stronger, more obvious way the Spirit leads is through the inner voice. This is not audible, but the inner awareness of a holy impression. This level of the Spirit's guidance can be frequent, but not so constant as level one.

There is a third, even stronger level of the Spirit's guidance which is much less frequent, but which can be very sacred. It is the level of inner compulsion by the Spirit (Acts 20:22). An example of this compulsive guidance is recounted in Mark 1:12: "At once the Spirit sent him out into the desert." "Sent" in the Greek is a very strong word that means "to cast forth, with the suggestion of force . . . hence to drive out or force."[10] It is the word normally used to describe how Jesus cast out demons.

This word suggests controlled guidance, with the Spirit gripping you. Warfield points out that it can even suggest "the

---

[9] Andrew Murray, *The Spirit of Christ* (Minneapolis: Bethany Fellowship, 1979), p. 128.

[10] W. E. Vine, *The Epistles to the Philippians and Colossians* (London: Oliphants, 1955), p. 332.

conception of the exertion of a power of control over the actions of its subject, which the strength of the led one is insufficient to withstand."[11] The New Testament uses this word many times in reference to animals, prisoners, the woman caught in adultery, the sufferers being brought to Jesus, and Jesus led to Pilate.

"Led by the Spirit," comments John Murray, "implies that they are governed by the Spirit (Rom. 8:14), and the emphasis is placed upon the activity of the Spirit and the passivity of the subjects."[12] Godet adds, "In the term '*agoutai*,' are led, there is something like a notion of holy violence: the Spirit drags the man where the flesh would fain not go."

In this level of guidance the Spirit drives us from within. "That is the glad testimony of those who have received the fulness of the Spirit. They are conscious of being projected on their course by the impetus of the Spirit." [13] Both Ezra and Nehemiah speak (six times) of the "gracious hand" of the Lord upon them. Isaiah and Ezekiel speak (eight times) of God's hand coming on them or His strong hand upon them, directing them as they prophesied.

You may not know guidance in the level of divine compulsion very often. But Christian biography confirms that Spirit-filled believers still experience this strong hand of the Lord. It is highly important to obey God's will in all such situations. The eventual effect upon your life and others may be very significant.

Similarly, the restraint of the Spirit in guidance can be felt at any of the levels, even at this strong level of inner compulsion. Undoubtedly this is what Paul experienced when he was "kept by the Holy Spirit" and when the Spirit "would not allow" Paul and his team to take certain journeys (Acts 16:6–7).

[11] A. Skevington Wood, *Life by the Spirit* (Grand Rapids: Zondervan, 1964), p. 71.

[12] John Murray, *The Epistle to the Romans* in *The New International Commentary on the New Testament* (Grand Rapids: Wm. B. Eerdmans, 1968), p. 295.

[13] Wood, *Life by the Spirit,* p. 72.

16

WAITING ON GOD FOR GUIDANCE

Prayer must be emphasized throughout our study of guidance. We must ask God specifically for a guided life and commit each day specifically to Him. Prayer is related to almost every step in guidance.

> If any of you lacks wisdom, he should ask God, who gives generously to all without finding fault, and it will be given to him (James 1:5).

> You do not have, because you do not ask God (James 4:2).

Often when we face a major decision we spend time weighing the pros and cons, try to gather information, and then in the final stages ask God to guide us in our conclusion. God does expect us to use all our fact-finding abilities, our reason, and our human resources. But God is our primary Guide, and our priority must be to seek Him first.

God Has No Emergencies

There are those wonderful experiences in life when a sudden crisis arises and almost instantly God gives the needed guidance. We prefer to have instant answers all the time, but that would not contribute to our spiritual well-being. The nature of guidance often requires extended time. You must allow God time to prepare you, others, and the situation for which you are praying.

Patience is always an important element in prayer. What is an emergency to you is never an emergency to God. He has foreseen the whole situation. God is never surprised. God is never without resources. God is never late.

Give God Time to Work

God has given every person the Godlike power of choice, the ability to think, react, and make up his mind. Since Adam, man has constantly been tempted to assert his independence from God. We stubbornly resist accepting what we have not ourselves chosen. God in His infinite patience gives us the permission to learn lessons the hard way.

In many guidance situations, the reactions of others is involved. God does not compel; He works with them, permitting their use of their own will and choice. Don't become impatient.

> You need never take a step in the dark. If you do, you are sure to make a mistake. Wait! Wait till you have light. Remind the Lord Jesus that as He is Counselor to the church of God, He will be, in your particular case, Counselor and Guide, and will direct you. If you patiently wait, believingly, expectantly, you will find that the waiting is not in vain, and that the Lord will prove Himself a Counselor both wise and good.   —*George Mueller*

1. Remember how patient God has been with you.

God may be exercising patience with you today in ways you do not realize. In fact, it may be primarily for your sake that waiting longer in prayer for guidance is important.

2. Remember that God may be more concerned with the opportunity of a situation than with the chronology.

God foresees when the situation is just right for the maximum result. That may be more important than the date or the hour on your clock. Your responsibility is to be ready and to make the most of the opportunity; give God time to get the situation ready.

3. Remember that only God knows the future.

Only God knows all the factors in the situation. Only He can coordinate all aspects at the most opportune time. Your part is to obey and to leave the future in God's hand. Let God be God. He will not procrastinate; God's time is always best.

Time waiting on God in prayer is never lost. From your perspective there may be much waiting and apparent delay. From God's perspective your waiting in extended prayer is investment.

Reasons Why You Need to Wait

1. Waiting on God enables you to know God better. To know a person you need to spend time with that one. To know God you must spend time with Him. The most precious knowledge in the world is the knowledge of God. After Moses had spent forty days with God on Mount Sinai he prayed, "You have said, 'I know you by name and you have found favor with me.' If you are pleased with me, teach me your ways so I may know you and continue to find favor with you" (Exod. 33:12–13). God granted his request. No one ever knew God face to face as Moses did (Deut. 34:10). And no one was given such detailed guidance as Moses. Waiting on God enables you to learn more and more of Him and His will.

2. Waiting on God teaches you spiritual lessons. God works not only *through* you, but more important, *in* you. Prayer helps you grow in grace, faith, and Christlikeness. God has important and blessed purposes to fulfill. Waiting on God places you in His school of grace. You become a better disciple as you wait.

Normally guidance becomes simpler and more natural as you go on with the Lord, but God may permit you to go through special faith-developing experiences. Sometimes you may pass through a period of darkness and testing. God is teaching you stronger, purer faith and courage. God is weaning you from dependence on your emotional feelings to naked faith in God. Hudson Taylor in his later years confessed that this was true in his life.[1]

3. Waiting on God strengthens your faith. Are you afraid to trust His provision and His time? Circumstances all around you may be in turmoil, but your heart can be at rest. Excessive haste may be an indication that you need to learn deeper lessons of faith. Trusting in God gives calmness and serenity. Trust delivers from feverish fretting, hectic struggling, and worry. The Hebrew of Isaiah 28:16

---

[1] M. Blaine Smith, *Knowing God's Will* (Downers Grove, Ill.: InterVarsity Press, 1979), p. 125.

reads, "The one who trusts will never be in a hurry." God may keep you waiting until you are absolutely sure of His will and have an unshakable faith and deep peace. Then you can move ahead with joy.

4. *Waiting on God develops self-confidence.* God may keep you waiting until your assurance of His will becomes deeper. By waiting on God you will become more sure of yourself and more decisive. This happened to Gideon (Judg. 6). You do not need to see the whole path before you begin the first step.

5. *Waiting on God develops a spirit of praise.* God often needs to teach you to praise. Guidance is easier as you love, worship, and praise. When you have prayed to the place of assurance, the petitions change to praise. Praise clears the way for guidance. Praise sometimes changes things unchanged by prayer alone.

When you don't know what to do, praise the Lord! When you fear the future, praise the Lord! When your decision is too big for you alone, praise the Lord! When your time for making the decision is growing short, you still have time to praise the Lord. Praise makes you available to God and God available to you.

Praise God that He is your loving Father who desires that you know His will. Praise Him for His promises of guidance. Praise Him that He is at work even when you cannot see it. Praise Him for the guidance He is going to give you. Praise Him for His faithfulness. Praise Him that He is now clearing the way before you.

6. *Waiting on God quiets your heart.* When your heart is not quiet, you may not recognize when God speaks. A busy mind often does not sense the mind of Christ. "My soul, be silent before God alone" (Ps. 62:5 Heb.). For hours before the Titanic struck the iceberg and sank with immense loss of life in 1912, other ships in the North Atlantic tried to give warning, but all the ship's radio lines were jammed with passengers talking to friends and relatives on shore. They were too busy to receive the warning messages.

Your heart can be so filled with thoughts, plans, memories, and worries that you fail to hear the gentle voice of God. Jesus instructed us that when we spend time in prayer we should go into our room and close the door (Matt. 6:6). A quiet heart is essential.

How can you clear your mind and close the door? Read God's Word until your heart is completely quiet and you sense only His presence and will. Perhaps it will help if you read Scripture aloud. Sing or read devotional hymns or choruses. I have at times read as many as fifty chapters from God's Word before I was completely alone with God. But on some of those occasions I received such unexpected guidance that my life has been greatly benefited.

7. *Waiting on God clarifies His impressions.* In a major decision God always gives you sufficient time to become sure. God's impressions are gentle, but as you wait before God, they become clear and strong. The longer you wait in prayer, the weaker Satan's distracting impressions become.

8. *Waiting on God makes you willing.* Unwillingness to do God's will should not be present if you are totally committed and Spirit-filled. But while God's will is being clarified, you may feel hesitation. In such circumstances, prayer is not overcoming God's reluctance but preparing your heart and will. It may take time to bring your desire and mood into harmony with God's.

9. *Waiting on God delivers from hurry.* A hurried spirit has difficulty hearing God's voice. Perhaps you are too anxious and nervous to hear what He seeks to say. God may need to slow you down long enough to gain full access to your heart.

10. *Waiting on God prepares for greater blessing.* God has greater plans than you have realized. Give Him time to do great things. The greater the work He plans, the greater the prayer preparation that may be necessary, including prayer for guidance. God often waits so that He can be even more gracious (Isa. 30:18).

11. *Waiting on God helps prepare others.* When you find God's will, others may be helped to discern His will for them. God's guidance to you may need to come at a time when it helps others too. Most questions regarding guidance have implications for others. God may need to prepare them also.

12. *Waiting on God may change your relationship with others.* A critical attitude, bitterness, carnal interpersonal attitudes, broken relationships, alienation and estrangement, unforgiveness—any of these can prevent your sensing God's nearness and smile of approval. These all hinder your prayers for guidance.

As you wait alone with God, He may point out aspects of your relationships that hinder. Examine your heart in the light of these Scriptures:

A critical attitude: Matthew 7:1–6; John 8:7; Romans 14:4, 10–15; 1 Corinthians 4:5–7; 2 Corinthians 12:20; James 4:11–12.

Anger: Psalm 37:8; Proverbs 15:18; 19:11; 22:21–25; 25:28; 29:22; Ecclesiastes 7:9; Jonah 4:4; Matthew 5:22; Galatians 5:19–21; Ephesians 4:26, 31; Colossians 3:8; 1 Timothy 2:8; Titus 1:7; James 1:19–20.

Bitterness: Acts 8:23; Ephesians 4:31; Hebrews 12:15; James 3:14–15.

Broken interpersonal relationships: Proverbs 17:14; Matt. 5:23–24. (Note you are responsible to act regardless of who is to blame, among family, church, or friends.)

Unforgiveness: Proverbs 24:17, 29; 25:21–22; Matthew 5:39–46; 6:12–15; 18:21–35; Mark 11:25; Luke 6:35–37; 17:3–4; Romans 12:14–21; 1 Corinthians 4:12; Ephesians 4:32; Colossians 3:13; 1 Peter 3:9.

13. Waiting on God may win spiritual warfare. Satan recognizes that if you are guided by the Spirit, great damage will result to his kingdom. Satan will do all he can to confuse, discourage, mislead, and keep you from receiving guidance. Prayer warfare may be necessary in obtaining God's guidance.

Daniel received God's special guidance in the form of a vision. He needed God to clarify the vision further and prayed and partially fasted for three weeks. Then Gabriel brought the answer. He told Daniel that his prayer was heard and granted the first day. But demonic forces fought against Gabriel until at last Michael came and helped defeat them (Dan. 10). If Daniel had stopped praying before the twenty-first day, he would not have received the guidance.

More spiritual warfare occurs in the heavenlies than you and I are aware of. You need not worry about that. Just keep waiting on God until He gives you the guidance you need or else tells you it is unnecessary. Over and over again, individuals and groups have stopped praying just before God's answer came.

the secret of listening

If you have not experienced divine guidance frequently, you may at first find more difficulty distinguishing the voice of the Lord from your feelings and impressions. You may feel unsure of yourself or of the Lord's desire or ability to communicate with you naturally and regularly. Usually the more you have experienced the preciousness of God's guidance, the easier it becomes to discern when He is speaking. There are several reasons for this.

1. *You develop a deeper hunger for continual guidance.* It becomes more of a priority, and you receive more because you ask more.

2. *You learn to trust God more simply and expectantly for His guiding voice.* The more He speaks to you, the more relaxed and confident you become. You rest in God's faithfulness.

3. *You develop a spiritual habit of listening.* Often you are almost unaware that you are listening. You become so restfully alert that, whatever the circumstances, you sense His slightest whisper, the glance of His eye, or the touch of His hand. Spiritual listening has become natural to you.

You do not question that He will guide you again. You know He is a speaking God and you develop the habit of listening. You are ready for the Spirit to guide you on any subject at any time. You have learned God is interested in even the smallest details of your life. You learn to take everything to Him in prayer, and listening for guidance becomes almost your second nature.

How to Develop a Listening Ear

You can develop a spiritual attitude and habit of listening for God's guiding voice. Any Spirit-filled Christian can develop this holy lifestyle. It will add new joy and meaning to your Christian life and service. You must be alert and attentive, but this will not be difficult or burdensome. It will lead you repeatedly to gratitude and praise to God. You will become more deeply conscious of God's fatherly care than ever before. I challenge you to try it.

1. Be filled with the Spirit. Be sure that you have made a total surrender to God and have been filled with His Spirit. You cannot trust for this if there is unwillingness on your part to accept God's will. Total commitment means *total* commitment. Hereafter you may be concerned at times to be sure you understand God's will, but there will be no serious struggle about doing it. You have said an eternal yes to God, and He is fully Lord in your life.

Donald Grey Barnhouse said, "I can say from experience that 95 percent of knowing the will of God consists in being willing to do it before you know what it is."

Your simple faith has opened your heart to the fullness of the Spirit. He has indwelled you ever since your new birth. Now He floods your life again and again with His presence. After the 120 were cleansed, empowered, and filled at Pentecost, they had further infillings as they had need (Acts 4:8, 31; 9:17; 13:9, 52).

As you serve the Lord you expend your spiritual energy and at times you may feel dry and depleted. But you have every spiritual right to ask God to refresh and refill you. Even Jesus sensed the expenditure of power as He ministered (Luke 6:19; 8:46). God promises times of refreshing (Acts 3:19). It is God's good pleasure that you live in the daily fullness of His Spirit.

When the Spirit fills you, He continually exercises His lordship through your surrendered will. It becomes comparatively easy for you to be motivated, restrained, or guided by the Spirit.

2. Ask God for a listening ear. In guidance, as in so much else, we have not because we ask not (James 4:2). Make this asking twofold. First, ask God to develop in you a listening ear. Second, from then on ask His guidance as you begin each day. You need not always express it in the same words, but the essence will be the same:

Lord, give me a listening ear today. Help me to recognize Your voice. Keep me alert and listening. Lord, I'm trusting You to guide me throughout today.

3. *Listen with expectancy.* To listen is to combine calm unhurriedness with quiet expectancy. Expect God's gentle touch, His slightest nudge or restraint. Go through your day expecting to hear His gentle voice at any time. Live in readiness, in constant availability, in moment-by-moment openness to God.

Prophets like Elijah (1 Kings 17:1; 18:15) and Elisha (2 Kings 3:14) testified that they "stood" before the Lord. The Hebrew word suggests standing in respect, obedience, and readiness to serve.[1] Just as the highest cabinet ministers stood in the presence of the emperor, instantly available to serve, so we too "stand" in God's presence at attention, alert, listening for any word from Him. What an honor to be available constantly to God!

4. *Remember that God speaks in many ways.* You may hear God at any time—during your quiet time, while you are busy at your duty, while attending a church service, while praying with or talking with friends, or even as you awaken. God may use a verse of a hymn, a passage of Scripture, a memory, or the counsel of a friend.

Above all, expect God to speak to you through His Word or prayer. Commitment to God's guidance involves commitment to continual reading of His Word. Read it prayerfully, regularly, and extensively. The more God's Word fills your mind and memory, the more easily the Spirit can use Scripture to guide you.

Observe how God guides, blesses, and works in the lives of others. One of the qualifications for a prophet was to be a close observer—of life, of the nation, of the people. "The LORD said to me, 'You have seen correctly'" (Jer. 1:12) has also been translated, "You are a close observer." As you prayerfully observe, you will sense God's will from many things.

5. *Begin to learn guidance in simple matters.* I suggest you begin with prayer. Ask God to give you a prayer assignment each day. "Lord, if someone is especially needing my prayer today, bring that

---

[1] R. Laird Harris, ed., *Theological Wordbook of the Old Testament*. 2 vols. (Chicago: Moody Press, 1980), II:674.

person to my mind. Put that one on my heart." Then trust God to guide you. Pray for that person in your free moments. Put the name beside your clock, on your refrigerator door, beside your mirror, or some other place where you will see it.

Snatch moments during the day to breathe a prayer for that one—while you are shaving, washing, doing dishes, driving the car, or waiting. If you can be free for two or three minutes, kneel beside your chair or bed, or sit quietly and pray.

The next day, ask God who should be your next assignment. It may be your pastor, a sick friend, a young person, a family facing problems, an unsaved neighbor, your senator, your president. It may be one of your loved ones, but be careful to focus most of your prayer concern outside your family circle.

I hope you make use of a written prayer list. God may put someone from that list on your heart. For example, one of my prayer lists names fifty-four persons who are imprisoned for Christ. I try to name each one briefly before the Lord daily. At times as I awakened in the morning, one of those names was instantly on my heart; it was God's special assignment for that day. Sometimes God may bring to your mind someone you have not thought of for months; accept that one as your prayer assignment that day.

Practice listening by asking God to show you those you can bless. God is a God who blesses. He is kind to the evil and the good. Jesus went around blessing others. He lived to bless. As Christians we should constantly bless others.

Ask God to open your eyes to people. It may be an older person with a package that you can carry. He or she may mention a need, and you can promise to pray. You may see a child who needs attention. You might say, "You have such a nice smile" or "You will soon be a big girl" or "You are really growing, aren't you?" Then add, "I hope you help lots of people as you grow up, and be sure to pray to Jesus," or a similar witnessing remark.

On Sunday ask, "Lord, make me a blessing in church today." Try to bless as many as possible with a loving smile, a cheery greeting, or a "God bless you." Pray for your pastor as he preaches and give him an encouraging word; thank the soloist. Be natural, but trust God constantly to show you ways to bless others.

6. *Learn God's guidance in daily activities.* When shopping, pray,

"Lord, guide me to any special bargain, but don't let me waste my money." At a public dinner or function, ask, "Lord, if there is anyone I should speak to, guide me." You may be amazed at the helpful information received after such a prayer. When traveling by bus or plane, pray, "Lord, if you want me to sit by someone today, work it out." God has arranged amazing contacts following such a prayer. Commit your work to the Lord:

Lord, if there is something I am overlooking, call it to my attention. Lord, how should I solve this problem?

Commit your driving the car, parking the car, phone conversations, letter writing, interpersonal family relations, relations with your neighbors or fellow workers, and other such items—commit them constantly for God's guidance.

Ask God to guide you in your citizenship—when to write your senator, mayor, or other political leader over an action of government, a proposed law, or civic problems. Ask Him to guide you in putting civic names and needs on your prayer lists for longer and shorter times. Ask Him to guide you in everything.

7. *Expect guidance to be natural.* Dramatic guidance is rare. Don't wait for the unusual to happen. Just be yourself, but keep trusting God to guide you, use you, and make you a blessing. Expect Him to bring a suggestion to your mind at any time. Also expect Him to quietly restrain you from any unwise word or action.

Don't expect an audible voice or vision. Just be relaxed, yet open and alert to any suggestion from the Lord, no matter how small it may seem. What may seem rather unimportant to you may prove to be very helpful or important to another.

8. *Thank the Lord each time He helps and guides you.* We all overlook many occasions when God guides. He may call something to your attention in the paper and impress you to fill your car's gas tank, and the next day the price goes up. Someone may "incidentally" mention an important bit of information. Breathe an instantaneous "thank you" to the Lord. You will find these occasions becoming more frequent. Thank Him.

As guidance becomes more and more a part of your spiritual lifestyle, God controls your life and uses you in ways more blessedly real than you ever dreamed possible.

9. Expect much of your guidance for the sake of others. Jesus lived a life of sacrifice for others. Today He wants to use your hands, feet, mouth, love, and talents. When you live in the will of God, you live for others. You owe them the blessings God has given you. You are now to present your body a living sacrifice to God by being totally His and totally available for others (Rom. 12:1–2). God wants to extend the influence of your love and your prayer until it includes many people. Begin by blessing those near you, but don't be content until your blessing extends as far as possible. God can guide your love, prayer, and obedience to bless a whole world. Why not?

Your primary motive in guidance is to please and glorify the Lord. Your secondary motive is to be a blessing to others. This corresponds with the two great commandments, as summarized by Jesus (Matt. 22:37–40): love to God and love to your neighbor.

We are members of one another. "Each member belongs to all the others" (Rom. 12:5). We are to have mutual concern for each other (1 Cor. 12:25). Next to the glory of God, we should be motivated by what will best serve and help others who need the touch of Christ's love.

Listening, then, should be more often for the sake of others than for one's own sake. Real *agape* love is to be poured out on others. "Nobody should seek his own good, but the good of others" (1 Cor. 10:24). Paul could testify, "I am not seeking my own good but the good of many" (1 Cor. 10:33). Beware of making your own interests your constant motive.

Seek God's way to bless others. Like Jesus, live for others. Then you will find that increasingly God will use others to bless you, bear your burdens, and benefit you in practical ways. This is God's law: "Carry each other's burdens, and in this way you will fulfill the law of Christ" (Gal. 6:2). Seek first God's priorities; then He will supply your needs, often even before you ask Him (Matt. 6:33).

10. Stay humble. God gives grace to the humble (James 4:6). Guidance is one of God's provisions of grace for you. Don't be quick to tell others how God guided. There will be times when it is appropriate to testify to God's guiding help. Share this with humility, Christlikeness, and joy. Remember how unworthy you are.

If you begin to become self-confident of your ability to hear

God's voice and take guidance for granted, God may have to withhold His guidance for a time. God will guide you when to share your testimony privately or publicly and when to keep it a sacred secret between you and Him.

11. *Stay available to God.* God may occasionally guide you so that you are in the right place at the right time to fill a very important role. God may suddenly use you in a way that has a very dramatic result. Don't expect that frequently, but when you live a guided life daily, God can alert you for special, urgent needs.

12. *Keep praising the Lord.* Praise draws you closer to God and makes you more conscious of Him. Praise helps you to be more submissive and dependent on Him. It fills you with anticipation and faith for His help. Praise helps you to let go and let God work.

Quiet praise helps your heart to rest and become so silent that you can hear God's voice more easily. A praising heart makes your companionship with the Lord more intimate and precious.

13. *Leave the responsibility with God.* Learn to rest in God's faithfulness in guiding you. He has more ways to guide you than you know to ask for. He sees possibilities you don't realize. A father is more responsible to guide a submissive, obedient child than that child is to ask. God assumes the responsibility when you are totally committed to Him, listening for His voice and resting on His sovereignty in your life. When you truly long to please Him, God is always ready to go the second mile to be sure you are guided.

18

YOUR GOD-GIVEN RESOURCES IN GUIDANCE

Because you and I are so precious to God and because it is so important in many of life's situations that we choose rightly, God has made wise provision for our assistance. "Every good and perfect gift is from above, coming down from the Father of the heavenly lights" (James 1:17). He is the Father of the stellar lights in the heavens—the sun and stars—and He is the Father of all moral light and truth. He is the Father of all true guidance.

God knows the perplexities of your life, the importance of your making right decisions, and your repeated need of information about others or the future. Scripture places a strong emphasis on wisdom, but wisdom always takes facts into consideration and depends on adequate information.

God has planned to give you the assistance you need. He has provided resources for major decisions so that you can live and decide wisely. Only a fool is too proud to admit his need of help, of information that he does not have. Only a fool is so independent that he refuses to use the resources available to him.

The Lord has provided three primary and four secondary sources of guidance.

Primary Sources of Guidance

1. *The Bible.* This is your most basic resource.
2. *The Holy Spirit.* He is your ever-present, all-wise Counselor.

3. The "mind of Christ." This the Spirit develops in you as you grow in spiritual understanding and maturity.

Secondary Sources of Guidance

1. Providential circumstances. Although in themselves they are inadequate and can be confusing, they often alert you to your need of guidance. The Spirit uses them frequently to confirm your guidance.

2. Your conscience. It is a part of your God-created personhood. When properly instructed, it is a great help in guidance.

3. The counsel of others. God often uses the comments or suggestions of other people to give you insight and information. Such advice is often more worthy of consideration if the person is a mature, wise Christian. It is usually better to get the advice of several people, especially if you are considering an important decision not covered by your primary resources in guidance.

4. Common sense. This is sometimes called sound judgment. It involves the innate ability to evaluate, discern, and arrive at wise conclusions. God gives this ability, but in some people it seems more reliable and less crippled by Adam's fall into sin than it does in others. Common sense can grow with experience, with training in careful thought and reasoning. It depends on careful observation, deliberate thought, and an unbiased power of reasoning.

All these secondary resources are God-given, but they must be informed and guided by the primary sources of your guidance. Each of these will be considered in some detail in succeeding chapters.

19

YOUR BIBLE IS
YOUR BASIC RESOURCE

The Bible is the primary resource for the Holy Spirit's guidance to you in the major decisions of life. The more your mind is saturated with the whole of God's Word, the more time you spend in daily reading and thinking on God's Word, the more prepared you will be for the Spirit to guide you in your crisis moments.

The Bible is especially important in your daily prayer time. You can pray often throughout your day, as you walk or drive your car or as you wait on someone. But it is more difficult to bring the Bible into your daily life except in the times you schedule alone with God. Normally the Christian should spend at least as much of his quiet time in reading the Bible as in prayer and intercession. Which is more important: your speaking to God, or your listening to God?

One reason many people know so little of God's guidance in daily living is that they have neglected God's Word. Your soul needs God's Word as much as your body needs daily food. Don't think that reading a page in a devotional book can take the place of God's Word itself. If you must choose between one or the other, choose the Bible.

If you read three chapters of Scripture each weekday and five chapters on Sunday, you can read from Genesis to Revelation in a year. You should never be so busy that you can't read the Bible that much. Yet some Christians read only parts of chapters or favorite chapters or favorite books of the Bible. What would you think if your friend read only certain paragraphs of your letter? You don't know the whole Word of God unless you read all of it regularly.

Make your main reading of Scripture consecutive. You are free to read from any passage God calls to your attention, but avoid reading mainly your favorite passages. To know God's Word, be familiar with the whole of it. You may read the New Testament more than the Old Testament, but remember that the Old was the only Bible Jesus had. You deprive yourself of much of God's truth and blessing if you read only from the New Testament.

Suggestions for Reading Scripture

1. Read your Bible consecutively as a normal practice. Set goals of how many chapters per day you will usually read.

2. Normally begin your private prayer time with Scripture. You will have fewer wandering thoughts if you read before you pray. Often prayer topics will arise out of your reading.

3. Give God priority time at the beginning of the day for the Word and prayer. You may be able to have a longer time later, but give God unhurried time before you begin your regular activities. There can be exceptions, but don't let most days become exceptions.

4. Plan to read God's Word at least as many minutes each day as you read the newspaper or watch a newscast. God's Word is far more important to you.

5. Keep alert to note how you can apply the Word to your life. Listen to God as you read.

6. Read extensively. While it is good to meditate upon precious selected verses, that does not take the place of extensive reading. You need the solid food of the whole Word, not just snacks. You do not get the Spirit's message through the writer's emphasis if the portions you read are too short. It is generally best to read several chapters at a time. It is good from time to time to read a whole book at a sitting, especially the New Testament epistles, so that you begin to sense the personality and the main emphases of the writer.

7. Store God's Word in your heart either by memorization or by constant reading. Once while ministering in South Africa, I learned that their prime minister purchased a new Bible each December so he would be able to mark a Bible afresh each year as he read it through. He found special blessing in marking and underlining. That year he was marking his thirty-first Bible.

While you need the light of Scripture in your major decisions and crisis moments, it also can play an important role in all your daily living. What does the Bible have to do with ordinary, daily decisions regarding family plans, interrelations with family or friends, problems at work, how you use your money and yet have money to give God His share? How does the Bible help in questions relating to your diet, your health, your phone calls, and your correspondence? Will your Bible habits make guidance more real and practical in details such as these? Most certainly. The more you saturate your mind with God's Word, the more it will come to your memory or unconsciously influence all your decisions.

The Bible is living and active, says Hebrews 4:12, penetrating your whole being. "It judges the thoughts and attitudes of the heart." The Greek word translated "judges" is *kritikos,* from which come "critic" and "critique." It suggests a sifting, investigating process. This is what the Word does. It searches to discover your motives and shines God's light on your thinking and attitudes. Thus it powerfully influences your actions and decisions.

Cautions Toward the Use of Scripture in Guidance

1. Beware of fanciful interpretations of Scripture. The plain meaning of Scripture, as understood by the average reader and in harmony with careful study of the Hebrew or Greek words involved, or as explained by good commentaries and as generally understood by church scholars, is what you must depend on.

But don't worry! You don't need to be a Bible scholar to be led by God's Word. The Bible is simple enough that the ordinary Christian can receive clear guidance through regular reading and meditation. Perhaps some would identify with Mark Twain when he humorously said, "It's not the parts of the Bible I don't understand that bother me, it's the parts I do understand."

2. Beware of understanding a verse in isolation and not in its full context. See the verses before and after. First understand a verse as the writer intended. Then you can make application to your current situation. General truths or general promises are easily applied to current situations. Be more cautious in applying verses originally given in highly specific situations. Occasionally God may bring to your memory a phrase from the middle of a section and you suddenly see how it sheds light on your decision; but use Scripture that way only with caution.

3. Beware of instant, hurried use of Scripture that is not based on daily reading of the Word of God. It is when the whole of Scripture is hidden in your heart from constant daily reading that its light shines brightest in your life. There are no shortcuts to guidance if you have been neglecting God's Word.

4. Beware of magical use of Scripture. You have heard of people who close their eyes, open the Bible at random, place their finger on a verse, and then look to see what God has to say to them! On very rare occasions God, in His mercy, may help a person in such a way! But to expect God to guide you regularly in such a way is not honoring to Him. Any neglect of God's Word in your daily life is dishonoring God by saying, in effect, "I am too busy to have time for what You have to say to me, God. I can't be expected to take my busy time and read the book You have inspired for me. Other things are more important in my life than Your Word."

I have found that most of the time when the Spirit uses Scripture to guide me, He does it in one of two ways: (1) either He reminds me of some Scripture verse, passage, or illustration, or (2) as I continue reading in the place where I have arrived in my regular, consecutive reading, I discover just what I need.

True, I may feel led to take a longer time alone with the Lord and thus may read many more chapters than I would otherwise read. Or I may be led to read a particular book of the Bible through at one sitting, or a major portion of a book, and then find what I need as I read. But God's Word to me is usually found right where I am reading at the time.

the spirit uses the bible to guide you

Your word is a lamp to my feet and a light for my path (Ps. 119:105).

The unfolding of your words gives light (v. 130).

All Scripture is God-breathed and is useful for teaching, rebuking, correcting and training in righteousness, so that the man of God may be thoroughly equipped for every good work (2 Tim. 3:16–17).

You must understand how the Holy Spirit uses His primary resource—the Bible—to give you guidance.

1. The Spirit can remind you of specific statements in the Bible that have some relation to a situation in your life.

2. The Spirit can remind you of Bible characters and what they did wisely or unwisely. Their examples may shed light on your situation.

3. The Spirit can remind you of Bible incidents that will have some relation to your situation.

4. The Spirit can bring to your memory Bible promises that will encourage you and give you guidance.

5. The Holy Spirit can use quantity reading of Scripture to quiet your heart and close the door so you can hear His voice more distinctly. Jesus said, "Go into your room, close the door and pray to your Father" (Matt. 6:6). You may have other ways to close "the door" and shut out your busy thoughts, your day's responsibilities, or other extraneous matters. Sometimes this can be done through reading hymns or quietly singing a hymn to the Lord. Perhaps you can do this by means of other devotional reading.

In my experience, on days of prayer when I know I am going to have a longer time with the Lord, I often read ten, twenty, or more chapters of Scripture—perhaps the Psalms or some portion of the New Testament. I finally have all other thoughts banished effectively from my mind. My heart is completely quiet and basking in the Word and God's presence. Often I become quietly aware that the Spirit is guiding my thoughts and speaking to me.

6. *The Spirit can develop biblical convictions in your heart concerning some types of action.* You learn what is right or wrong, wise or unwise, or needing special caution. These convictions may concern places you will or will not go, companions with whom you will or will not develop close associations, forms of recreation that you feel are not spiritually wholesome, types of literature you read or television programs you do or do not watch, what you do or don't do on the Lord's Day, and a host of other things. Some convictions may be positive and some, negative.

Just be careful not to demand that everyone else live according to your convictions. God has been patient with you; perhaps it took you a considerable time to develop some of your convictions. Be as patient with others as God has been with you. God probably has many new situations upon which He will give you holy convictions as you walk in His light (1 John 1:7).

7. *The Spirit can develop Bible principles in your mind that you will be able to apply to many situations.* These will help to answer many of your questions. Sample Bible principles include the following:

a. Christ owns me by creation and by purchase at Calvary. I am not my own (1 Cor. 6:19–20). I am only a steward of my life. I must live in such a way that I will not be ashamed when I stand before God and give an account of how I used my life.

b. I will reap what I sow (Gal. 6:7–9). Every thought I think, every act I do, can be an investment for eternity. I am sowing constantly. Therefore I can not only give joy to God, but also accumulate reward if I keep my thoughts pure and free from jealousy, resentment, critical feelings, and pride.

c. I should do to others as I would desire them to do to me (Matt. 7:12). This should guide my conversation about others, actions toward them, and prayer for them in times of need.

d. God's will supersedes the desires of family and friends when it relates to His calling me for service (Matt. 10:37– 38; Luke 9:59–62). I dare not disregard God's call in order to please others, no matter how dear they are to me.

8. The Spirit can illumine Scripture passages and apply them to your heart. Daniel was guided in his intercession (Dan. 9:2) by the prophecies about Jerusalem (2 Chron. 36:21; Jer. 29:10). David was guided not to harm Saul even when Saul sought to kill him, because Saul had been anointed king by God's direction. Even though he himself had been anointed to take Saul's place, David would not move his hand to speed up God's time (1 Sam. 24:5–6; 26:10–11). He would leave providence in God's hand. The ethics of many Christians are not as high as David's; they readily push others aside to gain advancement.

9. The Spirit can use Scripture to guide you in perceiving important distinctions that have significance for your decisions. "The word of God is living and active. Sharper than any double-edged sword, it penetrates even to dividing soul and spirit, joints and marrow; it judges the thoughts and attitudes of the heart" (Heb. 4:12). This is specially helpful in discerning personal motives that we otherwise might not recognize, except as the Spirit uses Scripture to search us.

10. The Spirit uses the Bible to preserve you from error. "Jesus replied, 'You are in error because you do not know the Scriptures or the power of God" (Matt. 22:29).

11. The Bible takes precedence over human counselors. Moses' father-in-law gave him good, general advice within the parameters God had stated, but added, "If you do this and God so commands, you will be able to stand the strain" (Exod. 18:23).

21

YOUR EVER-PRESENT COUNSELOR

The Holy Spirit is given to illumine you as He shines God's light on God's Word, God's will, and all of life. His major concern for you is spiritual; but you are a whole being, and God understands and loves you as a whole being—in all your relationships of home and family, job and fellow workers, church and society.

All that influences you, relates to you, and is of interest to you is of interest to God. You may be tempted to look on spiritual things as being especially sacred to God. They are. But all of your life has sacred meaning to God, and He desires to help make all of life to some extent sacred to you.

When God indwells you—His Spirit filling you, guiding you, and anointing you—He adds sacredness to your family joys, your work responsibilities, and your leisure hours. Whether you use your time for health, for mental or professional or spiritual growth, for helping others, for wholesome recreation, for family or church or neighborly fellowship, or for whatever is good or worthy or beneficial, the Spirit is present to guide and help.

All of the ministry of the Spirit is for all of your life. He is your *paraklētos*, your Companion-Counselor (John 14:16). Therefore you can trust for His guidance in any and every aspect of your life.

1. He is with you to guide you (John 16:13). In spiritual truth and doctrinal understanding, in spiritual growth, in Christlike service, and in prayer and the understanding of God's Word? Yes!

He is also with you to guide you in family plans, travel arrangements, workday decisions, financial planning and expenditures, and in all the multitudinous details of daily living. He is with you to guide you in your major crises and important decisions. He is also with you to guide you in the minutiae of life.

In Galatians 5:16 Paul urges us to "live by the Spirit." Two verses later he speaks of our being "led by the Spirit," and in verses 22–23 of our having "the fruit of the Spirit." Living in the Spirit is to give us a "Holy Spirit lifestyle." Then in verse 25 Paul sums up, "Since we live by the Spirit, let us keep in step with the Spirit." The words *keep in step* translate a Greek word meaning "to walk in a line, to walk in military formation, in battle order."

We must walk step by step behind the Spirit as He leads us. We are kept in line with each other and guided so as to be step by step in the will of God and marching forward for Jesus.

2. He is with you to teach you all things (John 14:26). To open up Scripture and illumine God's Word? to apply it to your own needs? to teach you the life of prayer and intercession? to teach you the deep things of God (1 Cor. 2:10)? Yes!

He is also with you to teach you more courtesy, neatness and cleanliness, wise use of your time, how to be a better parent, a better student, an effective church member, a more useful citizen.

3. He is with you to "remind you of everything" (John 14:26). Remind you of the words and example of Jesus? Scripture? spiritual lessons? the secrets of spiritual victory, commitments to God, and people? Yes!

He is also with you to remind you of your daily duties, of skills and professional training, of important information, of where you misplaced things, of people able to help you. What is there that would be unworthy of the Spirit's reminding you?

4. He is with you to anoint and enable you (2 Cor. 1:21; 1 John 2:20). To anoint and enable you in your praying, witnessing, and serving the Lord? Yes!

He is also with you to anoint you daily, for His anointing remains in you (1 John 2:27). The word *Christ* means "anointed." To be a Christian is to be an anointed person. Claim your privileges in Christ and begin to live under the Spirit's anointing.

The Spirit's anointing and special enabling are available to you for your daily activities. It can add a special dimension of guidance. He is life-giving, refreshing, and creative. He can bring new approaches to situations, creative solutions to problems, new ways to handle people, better ways to organize. Whatever your work, the Spirit's anointing can add a special dimension to your guidance.

Some years ago I was scheduled to address the Christian Medical Association of India. Just before I entered the session where I was going to speak on "The Anointing of the Spirit," I turned to one of my friends, a skilled surgeon.

"Ezra, is there such a thing as the anointing of the Spirit in surgery?" I asked.

Instantly my friend responded, "You bet there is, and I know when I have it and when I don't have it." The anointing can bring guidance to the surgeon as he operates.

Is there an anointing in teaching? in administration? There is. For the inventor? There is. Certainly the Spirit can anoint the research scientist to help him recognize insights and achieve an important "breakthrough."

There can be anointing on the mechanic, on the mother handling the children, on the secretary, the taxi driver, and the person learning a foreign language. I have recognized the anointing on occasion when driving in traffic. The anointing is for all. The anointing is for daily living, not just for the pulpit or the Christian writer. Remember, guidance is one aspect of anointing.

Since all of life can be holy and surrendered to God, all of it committed to His will, all of it lived in dependence on the Holy Spirit, the role of the Holy Spirit in your life is one of the most practical provisions of God for you. You can learn to live in the Spirit, to depend on the Spirit in all your daily living. Thus your life becomes transformed into a Spirit-guided, Spirit-anointed, and Spirit-enabled life.

the spirit will give
you wisdom

To make life's decisions and to relate to other people, you need wisdom. Every Christian has longed for more wisdom. You and I face many situations in life in which we urgently need wisdom beyond our own. The Bible recognizes our need, and many verses of Scripture speak to this need. Solomon said, "Wisdom is supreme; therefore get wisdom. Though it cost all you have, get understanding" (Prov. 4:7). Wisdom is a basic need in your guidance. How reassuring to know that God has made provision and that He Himself wants to be your wisdom!

The Bible recounts how God gave wisdom. God gave Joseph wisdom (Acts 7:10). David prayed for Solomon to be given wisdom (1 Chron. 22:12). Solomon prayed for wisdom and knowledge (2 Chron. 1:10), and the Bible records that God then gave him "wisdom and very great insight, and a breadth of understanding as measureless as the sand on the seashore" (1 Kings 4:29; see also 1 Kings 5:12; 2 Chron. 1:12). Solomon's God-given wisdom was evident in long-range planning as well as in administrative details. Daniel testified that God gave him wisdom (Dan. 2:23). God gives skill in practical details such as construction and craftsmanship (Exod. 28:3). What God did for those persons He is willing to do for you (Prov. 2:1–6, 10–12).

We need great wisdom in human relationships. Perhaps this is our most frequent, most urgent need. James 3:13–18 points out two kinds of wisdom. One is earthly and unspiritual (v. 15); the other is wisdom from above, supplied by the Holy Spirit (v. 17). Earthly wisdom is characterized by bitter envy, selfish ambition, disorder, and evil practices (vv. 14, 16). Godly wisdom is pure, peace-loving, considerate, submissive, full of mercy, full of good fruit, impartial, sincere, and humble (vv. 13, 17).

Your sanctified common sense is a form of wisdom from the Holy Spirit. He enables you to observe life, nature, events, and the lives of others and to draw observations and deductions from what you see. Just as He desires to give you a listening ear, so He desires to give you eyes that see, that discern God's hand in human events and the lessons God is teaching.

Your understanding of Scripture is a form of Spirit-given wisdom. God's Word is a lamp to your feet and a light for your path (Ps. 119:105). The unfolding of God's words gives light (Ps. 119:130). The Holy Spirit is given to us to illumine God's Word and apply it to our hearts and to our situations. The basic principles stated or illustrated in the Bible have light for most of the main decisions of life.

The Holy Spirit who anointed Christ is sent to be your wisdom. This is spelled out in detail in Isaiah 11:2. He is:

a. *The Spirit of wisdom.* The ability to help you fathom the essence and purpose of things; the ability to help you find the right means of achieving God's purpose.

b. *The Spirit of understanding.* The ability to help you discern circumstances, relationships, and people.

c. *The Spirit of counsel.* The ability to help you make right decisions, to inform and guide others.

d. *The Spirit of knowledge and fear of the Lord.* The ability to give you experiential knowledge of God (who He is, what pleases Him, and what He does), His will, and His ways.

In these ways the Holy Spirit's wisdom was given to Jesus and is given to us.

Christ is made our wisdom (1 Cor. 1:30). God's Word gives us wisdom (Deut. 4:6). Christ promises to give us words and wisdom (Luke 21:15). Paul speaks of treasures of wisdom available in Christ (Col. 2:3). He says these treasures are hidden, that is, we need the Spirit's help in searching them out. They are not ours automatically just because we are Christians. It is as we ask God for wisdom, and as the Holy Spirit fills and illumines us, that we receive Christ's wisdom in ever-increasing degree.

Paul's constant prayer for his converts was that God, the glorious Father, would give them the Spirit of wisdom and revelation (Eph. 1:17). Guidance often requires special wisdom, illumination, and revelation: "This is my prayer: that your love may abound more and more in knowledge and depth of insight, so that you may be able to discern what is best" (Phil. 1:9–10).

James adds, "If any of you lacks wisdom, he should ask God, who gives generously to all without finding fault, and it will be given to him. But when he asks, he must believe and not doubt" (1:5–6). *Ask* is in the present tense, i.e., go on asking, make it your spiritual habit to ask constantly.

God is not constantly finding fault with us; He does not blame us that we need wisdom. Wisdom for all our future is not given us in a moment. It comes as part of a process of repeatedly needing, asking, and receiving special wisdom from God. God does something better than giving us wisdom for all our future days in one package. He gives us the Holy Spirit as our divine Counselor so that He may guide us daily in wise choices. And this wisdom is available through constant prayer.

how the spirit speaks
to you

Have you learned to listen to the voice of the Holy Spirit? He does not usually speak audibly, although He spoke audibly to Moses and Israel at Sinai, to Samuel, to Paul on the road to Damascus.

God has at times spoken to people through angels, visions, and dreams. He did this more often before the writing of Scripture was completed and before the Scriptures were in the hands of the common people. He still uses these exceptional means occasionally. However, don't expect God to use these methods under normal circumstances. You now live in Christian light; you have the Bible, which you are to store in your heart (Ps. 119:11). You do not normally need spectacular methods.

Often the Spirit speaks through a hymn, a sermon, an event, or the counsel or word of a Christian leader or some other person. The particular means is impressed on your heart by the Spirit in a very clear and sacred way. Most commonly today the Spirit speaks to you through Scripture or through an inner impression.

Just as you do not need to pray audibly for God to hear you (1 Sam. 1:10–13), so the Spirit need not speak audibly for you to hear Him. His impression on your heart can be as clear as a voice. The Word of God is His voice to you.

The Spirit may speak gently like light falling on your pathway (Ps. 119:105). He may speak so directly and strongly to you that it is like a fire burning in your heart, or a hammer striking your heart

(Jer. 23:29). It may be like a sword penetrating your heart (Heb. 4:12). God more often uses the fire approach or the sword approach when you have been neglecting His Word or will.

The two primary ways to listen to the Spirit's voice are through His Word and prayer. Learn to hear the Spirit's voice in your Bible reading and by His inner voice. The Spirit will teach you a listening ear in both these ways.

Two Forms of the Spirit's Guidance

The Spirit's guidance consists in clear assignments and in helpful suggestions. Assignments are things that God wills for you. They are related to God's plan for you and His overall eternal purposes and plans for His people and the world.

God's helpful suggestions are gentle hints and suggestions that He gives to assist you. If you follow these, you will benefit physically, financially, vocationally, interpersonally, or in other ways. They help in commonplace, everyday matters.

God does not hesitate to assist even sinners in this way, but they are often not sensitive to His touch on their lives. God is a God of all grace and love. He desires good for all His creatures. Secular people speak of these touches of God's common grace as "hunches" and credit them to intuition. The Christian recognizes God's good hand in these moments. As Christians open themselves increasingly to God's guidance, these occasions may become much more frequent.

If you learn to sense these guiding hints or restraints, you will often save money or time and avoid problems. They can strengthen friendships or guide your speech. To miss or disregard these hints will not take you outside of God's will for your life, but you will lose advantages that God was ready to help you receive.

Just as you can practice the communing presence of God (a form and aspect of praying continually—1 Thess. 5:17), or just as you can cultivate a praising heart, so you can develop a spiritual lifestyle that looks to the Lord for guidance continually.

These two aspects of guidance are God's provisions for you. They blend together in the discussions in this book. At times my reference is to the Spirit's guiding in normal living. At other times my focus is on finding God's special will. The biblical teaching applies to both.

Suggested Steps in Learning to Listen to God's Word

Have you fallen into the habit of reading God's Word without applying it to your heart? God intended that His Word be personalized. The Bible is one of the Spirit's most important ways to teach you and to help you understand the heart of God.

All of Scripture is of value to you. If you neglect any part, you are missing blessing God longs to give you. However, the New Testament and Psalms contain special blessing for you. Expect God to say something personal to you as you read. Here are simple ways to learn to hear God's voice in His Word:

1. *Have a regular quiet place,* if possible, for your normal reading of God's Word and prayer. If this is not possible, ask God to show you how to shut out interfering noises and distractions. Going to the same place or using the same chair for your times with the Lord can help you get in spiritual quietness and expectancy.

Try to find a time when the children are sleeping or not around, or when others will know not to interrupt you. Some people who go to an office early to have their quiet time use a Do Not Disturb card on the door. Be sure to turn off your radio or television set when you read and pray.

2. *Pause* before you begin your quiet time. *Commit your time to the Lord* and specifically ask Him to speak to you.

3. *Keep a note pad* or sheets of paper and a pen with you. These will be useful to write down the thoughts God gives you about His Word and His will. Since you are expecting Him to guide you, be prepared to write down His suggestions as they come to you.

It is also useful to have a separate sheet of paper to write down other important thoughts. Because your heart is now quiet, you may suddenly think of a forgotten duty, someone's birthday, something you must tell a friend. Write it down briefly, and then go right back to the Word.

4. *Keep a journal notebook* for special truth God impresses on you in His Word, or guidance He gives. You may want to write down brief prayers of a sentence or two as you ask God to do in

your life or through you what you see and hear from His Word. Go back occasionally and read from your devotional journal.

5. *If you have an important appointment following your quiet time,* it will help keep your mind free if you *use an alarm watch or clock* to remind you when your devotional time is over.

6. *Shut the door of your heart* (Matt. 6:6). How do you shut your heart and mind to extraneous and intruding thoughts or ideas? Some find it helpful first to read or quietly sing in the heart a favorite hymn. Some find it helpful to read the Word audibly with a very soft voice. Hearing one's own voice shuts out other thoughts. Read at length if necessary, until other thoughts get shut out.

7. *Apply the Scripture you read to your heart and life.* Ask the Lord repeatedly, "Lord, is there some special light for me here? What are you saying to me? Is there something here I have never really understood? How can I benefit from this? Are You trying to show me something to pray about? Are You suggesting to me any assignment?"

But suppose you are reading a passage where you find nothing of special significance. Suppose it is a passage where you need someone to teach you before you fully understand it. Go on reading. Every time you read you are hiding God's Word in your mind and soul. The Word will be available, and sometime the Spirit may suddenly remind you of it so that it comes with freshness to you. God will reward you for being faithful to His Word even though your understanding of some passage is temporarily limited.

8. *Distinguish between God's voice and your own impressions.* The Holy Spirit's quiet inner voice often comes in the form of holy inner impressions. But you can receive other impressions as a result of your own feelings, emotions, and thoughts. Mentally unstable people have hallucinations and imagine voices. Satan does not hesitate to mislead by tempting thoughts and suggestions. People who have been involved with the occult tell of hearing the voices of evil spirits. Satan may try to bring these back after your conversion. Resist him in Jesus' name.

24

IMPRESSIONS – IMPORTANT OR DANGEROUS?

An impression is an inner suggestion, prompting, or influence on your mind. It influences your opinion, purpose, feeling, or action. Impressions may be positive or negative.

Your impressions come from many sources. Your mood, health, some forms of medication, your surroundings, associates, the weather, childhood memories, the acts or remarks of other people, your own strong likes or dislikes—all will influence how you act or react. Often you are influenced by many factors that you do not realize. You need to identify the things that strongly impress you so as to become more mature.

Your inner intuitions and impressions are only as valid as the information to which you have been exposed and your own attitudes and prejudices. Your personal desire may strongly influence them. Your impressions may tell you more about yourself than about the circumstance. Impressions must be carefully investigated before they are accepted. Check your impressions by facts and objective standards as far as possible. What lies back of your impressions?

God gives you many practical inner suggestions and moral and holy impressions. These are given you by the Holy Spirit. The Spirit's voice occasionally comes as a sudden impulse or restraint. Often, however, it comes as a gradually deepening conviction.

Paul reminds us, "It is God who works in you to will and to act according to his good purpose" (Phil. 2:13). The Spirit helps you choose what to say or do. This we often call the "inner voice." Most impressions today come in the form of an inner suggestion or restraint (John 16:13).

In 1940, E. Stanley Jones was in India, needing to come to the United States. As he prayed, "the Inner Voice assured me . . . 'I'll get you there safely and on time.'"

Every booking he tried proved impossible. Finally He went to Bombay and got a ship to New York via Cape Town, South Africa. It would take forty days—and that would make him late for his appointment. But there was no alternative.

In Cape Town the ship was detained for three days. While en route, the ship was ordered to stop in Trinidad. There Jones caught a plane to Miami, flew on to Chicago, and started for Michigan by car. Within twenty miles of his destination, the car broke down. After three hours of hard work, it was repaired enough to travel again. He arrived at his destination as the church bell for the opening service was ringing. He had arrived "safely and on time." Said Jones, "The Voice did not let me down. Across the years it has never let me down."

We find an example of the Spirit's inner voice in Acts 15:28. "It seemed good to the Holy Spirit and to us," said the apostles. Archbishop William Temple often felt an inner impression to call on people and then found he could be of special help to them in a time of need.[1] These occasions became much more rare, he confessed, if the closeness of his fellowship with the Lord decreased or if he had grieved the Lord in any way.

Mrs. Commissioner Norman Marshall of the Salvation Army was suddenly strongly impressed to phone her widowed mother, who lived across the country in Los Angeles. As she spoke to her mother, she said, without realizing she was being guided, "Mother, would you like me to fly out west? We'll have a good visit together." Her mother wanted this very much.

Not realizing why, Mrs. Marshall felt impressed to leave immediately, which she did. On arriving, she found her mother in

---

[1] Leon Morris, *Spirit of the Living God* (London: Inter-Varsity Fellowship, 1960), pp. 79–80.

bed and very tired, with no appetite. She arranged a doctor's appointment for the next morning, and he in turn arranged for blood tests. Three hours after the tests he called to say that Mrs. Marshall's mother had leukemia and could pass away at any moment! Amid the state of shock, the two women had loving conversation together, and four and a half hours later the mother slipped into heaven. How important that we know how to recognize the inner voice!

Many others can testify to the same truth. The closer your walk with the Lord, the more likely you are to receive His gentle, guiding touch or His inner voice. If this is less frequent than before, examine your love for the Lord to see if it has cooled from neglect or disobedience.

How Satan Impresses

Satan tries to use the same means of guidance as the Holy Spirit uses. His impressions we call "temptation." He has used dreams as much or more than God has done (Deut. 13:1–3; Jer. 23:25–29; 29:8–9), but it is as chaff compared with wheat. Dreams are most of the time meaningless—related to our physical condition, our work and activities, or our thought life (Eccles. 5:7).

Satan uses circumstances to try to misguide as he did in the case of Job and in the case of Paul's shipwrecks and other sufferings (2 Cor. 11:25). Sometimes God permits Satan to manipulate situations temporarily. Satan often speaks through sinners, good-intentioned people, and even at times through Christians without their being aware of it (consider the example of Peter in Matthew 16:23 or Paul's friends in Acts 21:12–14). Be careful, or Satan will try to use you in giving misguided advice to others.

Above all, we need to beware of Satan's seeking to counterfeit the guidance of the Spirit through the inner voice. He delights to deceive people by masquerading as an angel of light (2 Cor. 11:14). He does not hesitate to quote Scripture and interpret and apply it in a wrong way (Matt. 4:1–11). John Wesley said,

> Do not hastily ascribe things to God. Do not easily suppose dreams, voices, impressions, visions, or revelations to be from God. They may be from Him. They may be from nature. They

may be from the Devil. Therefore believe not every spirit, but
"try the spirits whether they be from God."[2]

Satan will seek to plunge Christians into confusion and despair
through false accusations. He is the "accuser of our brothers" (Rev.
12:10). In fact, his name, *Satan,* means "accuser." He will accuse of
worthlessness, failure, and sin. He is the author of discouragement,
hopelessness, and suicide.

Satan will accuse God, insisting that God does not love you
anymore because you have failed. He will accuse Christ of being a
hard Master. He will accuse Christians of having so missed God's
guidance that opportunity is past. He hides the fact that Christ will
take you wherever you are, transform your life, and open a whole
new set of opportunities.

Satan accuses one Christian to another. He uses false accusations about motives and false charges that others deliberately ignore
you. He is constantly sowing dissension. Jesus called Satan "a liar
and the father of lies" (John 8:44). Satan's demons are deceiving
spirits (1 Tim. 4:1).

The Devil is the author of all false prophecy, for he deceives
those who foretell through astrology, séances, and all forms of the
occult. The use of any method to foretell the future apart from
God's Word or God's prophet is strongly condemned throughout
Scripture.

> Let no one be found among you . . . who practices divination or
> sorcery, interprets omens, engages in witchcraft, or casts spells,
> or who is a medium or spiritist or who consults the dead.
> Anyone who does these things is detestable to the Lord (Deut.
> 18:10–11).

Any true information provided through any of these means is but a
satanic bait to win your confidence and then plunge you into many
deceptions.

No informed Christian will attempt to discover the future
through any means except Scripture or prayer. Astrology, crystal
gazing, palmistry, fortune telling, reading tea leaves, tarot cards, or

---

[2] Martin Wells Knapp, *Impressions* (Cincinnati: Revivalist Publishing House,
1892), p. 34.

any other form of divination are contrary to both the Old and the New Testaments. They are abominable in the sight of God (Deut. 13:12). If you have participated in any of these, receive the Lord's forgiveness and cleansing as from any other sin, renouncing it forever.

Inner temptations are satanic impressions that he brings to your mind. Don't be surprised by them, for even Christ was tempted by Satan "in every possible way" (a legitimate translation of Luke 4:13). No doubt most of Satan's temptation of Christ was by inner impression. You need not be fearful of temptation. God promises to help you be victorious (1 Cor. 10:13).

Among the many ways in which God will guide you will be good and helpful impressions that He brings to you. He wants to use impressions and other gentle forms of guidance to lead you joyfully and in perfect rest of heart as you realize more and more the wonder of His intimate personal love for you.

you can distinguish impressions

Can you learn to recognize the voice of God? Certainly! Jesus said that when the shepherd leads the way, the sheep follow him "because they know his voice" (John 10:4); but they will not follow a stranger, because they do not recognize his voice. Again, "My sheep listen to my voice" (v. 27).

The more you fellowship with someone, the more easily you recognize their voice. It is almost impossible to describe, yet very knowable. The same is true with the voice of the Spirit. The more you listen to Him in the Word or in prayer, the more familiar you become and the more certain you are when He is speaking.

1. God's voice is quiet and gentle. Other impressions may be loud, clamorous, feverish, harsh and strong. God persuades; He does not drive. He leads you.

2. God's voice is loving and patient. Other impressions may be impatient and demanding.

3. God's voice gives you time to understand. Other impressions try to rush you and make you impetuous. Any impression that makes you impatient is not of God. The Spirit always gives you time to pray and consult.

4. God's voice gives strength and encouragement. Other impressions tend to question, discourage, or lead to despair.

5. God's voice is often accompanied by a sense of His sacred nearness, His goodness, and His love.

6. *God's voice speaks and leaves you with a sense of His peace and the assurance that you have pleased the Lord.* God does not pester you. Satan's voice nags, pesters, threatens, and gives you a sense of foreboding and fear rather than peace and assurance. He puts you under strain and pressure.

7. *God never suggests anything that is unholy, unethical, morally questionable, or unlike Christ.* God's voice never impresses you to do anything that might bring dishonor to Christ or you.

8. *God's voice never impresses anything that is contrary to Bible teaching.* God's Word is always the final test. Satan's voice seeks to make you think your situation is an exception to the Bible.

9. *God's voice leads you to take action in harmony with His providence.* He puts His seal as you obey by providentially opening doors for you. When God is guiding, you never have to break open a closed door. The door may seem closed, but as you obey, God opens the way as He did for Joshua at Jordan.

Satan urges you to go contrary to providence, to do even outlandish things, to be excited and take daring risks that mature Christians will feel are contrary to God's will.

10. *God's voice makes you considerate of others* (Phil. 2:4). He never leads to do anything that might harm or mislead others. Satan urges you to demand your rights, to feel mistreated. He makes you inconsiderate. He focuses your attention upon yourself with thoughts of self-pity and self-assertion.

11. *God's voice always leaves you feeling humble and unworthy of God's speaking to you and using you.* "He guides the humble in what is right and teaches them his way" (Ps. 25:9). Contrariwise, Satan's voice makes you feel important, special, and deserving of the attention of others.

12. *God's voice always respects your selfhood, your personality, your body.* God never depreciates you. He may convict you of sin or reprove you, but always with love and hope and promise.

13. *God's voice is always in harmony with sanctified common sense.* If God asks you to take some major step of obedient faith that others might not understand, He is always willing to give you additional confirmations. These may take the form of comments of godly people, special providential circumstances, and deep inner peace.

The Promise of God's Voice

God takes the responsibility to speak to you for you are His child. When you are filled with His Spirit you can expect Him to speak to you. Satan wants to make you fearful, worried, and indecisive. He would like to rob you of the assurance and joy of guidance.

Isaiah gave prophetic and spiritual encouragement to Israel in Isaiah 30:19–21. It was literally true for them, but it is a general spiritual truth. God always wants to act for His people, be gracious to them, answer when He hears them, and guide them so they will not make a mistake. Read the whole passage, but note specially verse 21: "Whether you turn to the right or to the left, your ears will hear a voice behind you, saying, 'This is the way; walk in it.'"

This points to the nearness of your Teacher and to your sensitivity to His guidance.

> Here is a person whose teacher is just at his shoulder and little more than a word of guidance from time to time is necessary for him to stay on the right path. This is the ideal of the Spirit-filled life, where the contact between us and him is so intimate that only a whisper is sufficient to move us in his way (Gal. 5:16–25).[1]

Is this not implied by Galatians 5:25? "Since we live by the Spirit, let us keep in step with the Spirit."

Isaiah 30:21 can be interpreted two ways. Perhaps it means that when you are walking in God's will and need to change directions, you will hear the Spirit's voice pointing to the right or to the left. Perhaps, however, it means that as you walk in the light as obediently as you know how, should you be about to make a mistake, leaving the center of His will, the Spirit will instantly speak to you. Whether you are about to turn right or left, the Spirit will gently point you back, saying, "This is the way; walk in it." Actually I believe both interpretations are wonderfully true.

Isn't this blessed! When you are listening for God's voice and need direction or restraint, the Spirit will take the responsibility to

---

[1] John N. Oswalt, *The Book of Isaiah*, Chs. 1–39, in *The New International Commentary Series* (Grand Rapids: Wm. B. Eerdmans, 1986), pp. 560–61.

speak. Relax! God loves you! You are His child! To be led by the Spirit is your birthright (Rom. 8:14). He will not fail you. He takes the responsibility. He is far more desirous that you find God's best than you are to know and do what is best. You could misunderstand or forget—He can't. He will speak. As surely as He is God, He will keep His promise. Rest in His faithfulness. He will speak to you.

In 1873, before the days of radio, the ship *Ville de Havre* sailed from New York. She was struck by the ship *Loch Erne* and sank in eight minutes. Some survivors were saved by the *Loch Erne* and some by the ship *Trimountain,* which soon sailed away. The next day *Loch Erne* began to sink. The steering became disabled, and a strong wind blew the ship far out of the normal lane where the Atlantic vessels traveled. Each day the ship settled lower in the water, and finally the captain announced that the ship would sink within a day.

On board was a godly minister by the name of Cook. After long hours of prayer he announced that God had assured him all would be saved. By morning, the passengers were standing knee-deep in water and expecting the ship to take the final plunge to the bottom at any moment. Suddenly the *British Queen* hove into sight, and all were rescued. What was the secret?

The night before, the captain of the *British Queen,* who was a Christian, felt impressed that there was special work for him to do, someone to save. He felt led to turn the ship in a more northerly direction. Then he heard the inner voice say, "Steer north." He turned the ship still further north and ordered that the vessel go at top speed all night. At the crack of dawn, the lookout called, "Ship ahead!" There lay the *Loch Erne.* God had a Christian who discerned the voice of the Spirit, and all lives were saved!

How God Confirms His Inner Voice to You

1. God may give you a strong inner sense of duty, a holy compulsion in harmony with spiritual concerns. He helps you feel the importance of your doing His will.

2. God may give you a deep spiritual hunger and longing, a desire to do your best and to be of loving service.

3. God may repeat the impression with ever deepening but quiet conviction that this is of God.

4. God always accompanies His voice and impression with a deep sense of peace and/or joyful assurance.

5. God helps you realize how you can give yourself, not how to gain advantage at the expense of others.

6. God may cause a Scripture portion or verse suddenly to grip you. Usually not when you hunt for a special verse; rather, it comes while you are reading your Bible normally.

7. God may give you a strong inner confirmation as you hear a remark of another person, or He may apply to your heart some comment you hear in a sermon or song.

8. God may develop a deepening restlessness and apprehension about something you have been doing or planning.

9. God may bring a persistent questioning about the wisdom of an action or the timing of an action you contemplate.

10. God may grip you with a sudden sense of danger that alerts you or that causes you to change your plan of travel or that calls you to prayer for whatever guidance God then gives you.

11. God may give you a special drawing to prayer and then unfold suggestions to you or guide you in intercession for others.

12. God may occasionally confirm His will to you through some "fleece." (See appendix B.)

God speaks to us in more ways than we can possibly enumerate. As you walk with Him, He will make you more and more experienced in listening to His voice, and you will experience increasingly the joy of a God-directed life.

thrilling examples
of guidance

I have been emphasizing how naturally and normally God can guide us, not only in our prayer and spiritual life, but also in our daily living and work. Yet God also delights to guide us in special times of need. Christian biography and missionary accounts are filled with outstanding examples. Let me share a few.

Guidance in Travel and Ministry

After Bishop James M. Thoburn began a ministry in Calcutta, India, in 1874, God opened up contacts and invitations to begin Methodist work in Rangoon, Burma. After five years of waiting for God's guidance, Bishop Thoburn was led to take a small group of Christian workers to Rangoon. They had to borrow money to pay for their ship passage. The bishop preached twice daily for two weeks and at the end of that time had organized a church of more than sixty members, had been given a free plot of land on which to build the first church, had begun street preaching in three languages, and had enough money to repay the loan.

Five years later, Thoburn felt God's heavy burden to leave Calcutta and begin Methodist ministry in Singapore. Again he started out by faith, but with the same strong sense of guidance as before. He stopped by the new church in Rangoon, where the congregation took up offerings and paid his way and three others' to Singapore.

When the little group stepped ashore in Singapore, a man named Charles Phillips stepped up, introduced himself, and said the party of four were to be his guests. Thoburn asked in astonishment how Phillips knew anything about them. Phillips answered that during the night God gave him a vision telling him the group would be arriving on that ship and showing him the faces of the four people so clearly that he recognized them instantly at the dock. God worked mightily in the establishing of that Methodist work![1]

Guidance Concerning Property

At a prayer meeting in Calcutta in May 1890, Bishop Frank W. Warne gave a message entitled "Greater Works Than These Shall Ye Do." While a saintly woman prayed, Bishop Warne relates, he

heard a voice saying to me, "Ask for the property in Jaun Bazar and it shall be given you, and through that the 'Father will be glorified in the Son.' " With the hearing of that voice I received a most joyful consciousness that God had spoken to me, even me, as He had to the prophets and apostles. The joy of that hour made Paul's experience "Whether in the body or out of the body I cannot tell" much more understandable, and through many days that followed my joy was unspeakable.

The bishop had been praying for months for this valuable piece of property. It took several years, during which his faith was often severely tested, but he held onto God's promise as spoken to him in clear guidance, and now for years this has been a center of ministry—the property now worth millions of rupees.[2]

Another Guidance About Property

The early Methodist missionaries in Lucknow, India, from 1887 on, searched and searched for a suitable plot of ground on which to build what is now Lucknow Christian College. B. H. Badley always spent half an hour in prayer each morning at five o'clock. One morning while he prayed with closed eyes and bowed head, God helped him see suddenly a large thirty-five-acre plot that

---

[1] Frank W. Warne, *A Prayer-answering Christ* (Madras: Madras Publishing House, 1932), pp. 18–19.
[2] Ibid., pp. 27–28.

was a huge "tank" (a manmade pond used as a water source). Dr. Badley asked the Lord, "What can we do with that tank?" God's inner voice said, "Fill it in."

Badley rose to his feet and said, "I thank Thee, Lord." He then called three colleagues, and each in turn prayed for God's guidance. They went that morning to the office of the Secretary to the Government. He immediately "welcomed them and their request as though he expected them and wanted to comply with their desires." Within a month they got word that the government would give that land to them free of cost for the purpose of founding the college.

In 1905, George, Prince of Wales, and Princess Mary came to India and visited Lucknow. The government decided to build a hospital and medical college in honor of their visit. It wanted the best site in all of Lucknow for the purpose and decided to take the property that had been given to the missionaries for the college. The college president, C. L. Bare, called a small group together, and they spent a long time in prayer for divine guidance. Almost immediately they were informed by the government that it no longer wanted the property! God's guidance to Dr. Badley had been perfect, and the valuable property is being used for the college to this day.[3]

Guidance in Ministry

My friend, Duncan Campbell, a minister of the United Free Church of Scotland, Edinburgh, was mightily used of God in the Hebrides revival in the late 1950s and 1960s. He has shared with me outstanding examples of God's guidance, the power of prayer, and God's deep working in true revival and spiritual awakening. Further accounts can be found in his biography.[4]

On the Monday after Easter in 1952, Duncan was seated on the platform after speaking in the Faith Mission Convention in Bangor, Northern Ireland, when he sensed the inner voice say to him, "Berneray!" Duncan bowed his head and prayed silently. Again came the name "Berneray." He prayed on, and the name came a third time. Duncan turned to the chairman and said,

---

[3] Ibid., pp. 30–32.

[4] Andrew Woolsey, *Duncan Campbell* (London: Hodder and Stoughton, 1974).

"Brother, you will need to excuse me. The Holy Spirit has just told me that I am to go to Berneray."

"Why, brother," the chairman replied, "you can't go there. You are the speaker again tomorrow."

"But what must I do? The Spirit says, 'Berneray,'" Duncan responded.

"I guess you'll just have to obey the Spirit."

Instantly Duncan walked off the platform while the service was continuing, and he went to the hotel where he had been staying. "Remember," he told me later, "I had never been to Berneray, had never known anyone from there, and had never received a letter from anyone there."

Duncan packed his two suitcases, took a taxi to the airport, and asked for the first plane to Berneray. He was told there was no air service to this small island in the Outer Hebrides. "Well," Duncan said, "put me on the first plane to the nearest point." He flew across the channel to the nearest airport, went down to the seashore, and asked a fisherman, "How can I get to Berneray?" The man responded that there was no regular means available, but he would be willing to take him in his boat. Duncan asked how much it would cost. The man named a figure that was almost the exact amount Duncan had in his pocket. When Duncan disembarked from the fishing boat at Berneray, the fisherman immediately returned whence he came.

Duncan was unable to see over the bluff. He climbed up, dragging his suitcases that were heavy with books. He found himself in a plowed field and, seeing the farmer up ahead, he approached him and sat down, exhausted, on one of the suitcases.

"Please go to the nearest pastor," Duncan requested, "and tell him Duncan Campbell has arrived."

"Oh," said the young farmer, "we don't have a minister for the church now."

"Do you have elders?" Duncan asked.

"Yes," came the reply.

"All right," said Duncan, "go to the nearest elder and tell him, 'Duncan Campbell has arrived.'" The farmer looked at him quizzically, then started off across the field. Duncan sat resting on his suitcase.

After a while the farmer returned and told Duncan, "The elder was expecting you. He has a place ready for you. He has announced the meetings begin at nine o'clock tonight! Here, let me carry your suitcases."

While Duncan had been ministering in the convention at Bangor three days earlier, this elder had spent the day praying in his barn for God to send revival to the island. God gave him the promise in Hosea 14:5: "I will be as the dew unto Israel." He claimed it in faith. His wife in the house heard him praying in the barn, "Lord, I don't know where he is, but You know, and with You all things are possible. You send him to the island." He knew in his heart that God was going to send Duncan Campbell, who had been used in mighty revival in other parts of Scotland, to Berneray. He was so sure that Duncan would be there in three days' time that he made all the arrangements to use the local church and had announced the services.

The account of how God sent revival to Berneray is a thrilling story, of which this is only the first part. When God has people who prevail in prayer, and people who know how to recognize the voice of the Spirit and obey without question, there is no limit to what God can do.

Guidance in Danger

During the Korean conflict in 1950, when the Chinese joined the war and moved south from North Korea, thousands attempted to flee before the advancing Communist armies. Among these was a godly Bible woman named Yu Eul Hee. She worked under the Korea Evangelical Church (founded by OMS International). Like many others, her heart of love had reached to the orphans and refugee children, and one by one she took them until she had some forty in her home. When the flight south began, she took her children, ranging in age from toddlers to teenagers, the older ones helping to carry and escort the younger. They walked by day and sheltered where they could by night.

One night Yu Eul Hee and her group reached a village where they were offered shelter by a kindly old man whose family were gone. After devotions with the children, she committed them all to the Lord for the night, and they bedded down on the floor. At about two o'clock in the morning she was awakened by the Lord with a sense of imminent danger. The inner voice of the Lord told her to take the children at once and leave. She awakened the children and the old man, but he refused to accept her warning.

The group went several hundred yards and found shelter beneath a large tree and bedded down again, this time on the ground. Suddenly a bomb fell on the house where they had been sheltered and completely destroyed it. The people in the surrounding houses gathered around the smoldering ruins, weeping and searching for the bodies of the children; they knew the orphans had sheltered there that night. Yu Eul Hee called out to the people not to weep, for the children were all safe. She testified how the Lord had guided her to safety.

As Yu Eul Hee told me this and other stories of how God had supplied all her needs and guided her from place to place during the tragic months of the war and over the years that followed, she patted my hand, praising the Lord. She had established and managed three orphanages since that time, with hundreds of children, and was trusting the Lord for all her needs. Again and again God had guided her and provided for her. For all these years God was her chief Counselor.

the spirit
will restrain you

The Holy Spirit not only delights to give you inner suggestions, but also shows you what not to do, say, or even pray. He restrained Paul in his prayer (2 Cor. 12:7–9). If you train yourself to listen and keep sensitive to the Spirit, you will find His restraining very real and blessed and frequent. The restraints of the Spirit are as important as the suggestions and urgings of the Spirit.

The restraining ministry of the Spirit is an important aspect of God's providential government of the universe. It is part of the manifestation of God's grace to mankind. To the Holy Spirit is committed the responsibility for this role, in which He is assisted constantly by the angels of God. The Spirit restrains Satan, the demons, sinful mankind, and even at times children of God.

The Restraining Guidance of Christians

The restraining ministry of the Spirit is as much a token of God's love as the encouraging and comforting ministry. The restraint of the Spirit may be as important in keeping you in the center of God's will and effectively guided as His suggesting ministry. When God led Israel from Egypt to Canaan, the times when the cloud and pillar of fire moved forward and the times when it stopped were equally significant. "At the LORD's command the Israelites set out, and at his command they encamped" (Num. 9:18).

George Mueller said, "The stops of a good man, as well as his steps, are ordered by the Lord." Christ promises to use His key both to open and to close doors before you (Rev. 3:7–8). An open door is no more important than a closed door. Both may be divine guidance, or neither. More important than doors is the urging or restraining of the Spirit. Guidance without either is incomplete.

Bona Fleming had to change trains in Cincinnati and St. Louis to reach his evangelistic engagement in Oklahoma. As he waited in the Cincinnati train station, an inner voice impressed him, "Don't take that train." Fleming argued in his mind, "This is the only train sure to make connections for the westbound train." Again the inner voice spoke, so clearly that Fleming turned around to see who had said, "Don't take the 9:30 train." No one had spoken. He began to sense impending danger.

Just before the 9:30 train was announced, Fleming thought, "I must get there in time for that meeting. I do not want to disappoint the people." "Leave that to me," came another clear impression. Fleming paused a bit, then doubting his impressions he started up a third time. Again the clear impression came: "Don't take that train!" Fleming went back to his seat. As he waited he felt an abiding sense of peace.

Fleming boarded the noon train. Ninety miles out of Cincinnati, the train stopped. There on the siding they saw the wreckage of the 9:30 train. When Fleming reached St. Louis, he made the proper connections and reached his Oklahoma engagement on time.

Some of God's restraints in your life may be dramatic and may involve major decisions. Others may be built into your life so naturally that you are as unconscious of them as you are of some of God's touches of prompting. Both can become as normal in your spiritual life as eating or exercising are in your physical life.

Why the Spirit May Restrain You

1. *The Spirit may restrain you temporarily so you will await God's time, God's person, or God's fully prepared situation.* Further guidance will come to you as situations develop and as God brings other people into your life. When the Spirit restrained Paul from going to Asia, he could not go to Ephesus. Yet later, on Paul's third

missionary journey, God used him mightily in Ephesus for three years.

2. The Spirit may restrain you temporarily as a part of His training for you. God teaches you the secrets of the guided life both by His suggestions and by His restraints. When Paul finished his evangelistic campaign in Phrygia and Galatia, why did the Spirit not immediately guide him to Macedonia? Perhaps to teach Paul how to develop a listening ear sensitive to the whispers of the Spirit. Paul was being taught total dependence in guidance. Undismayed, he pressed forward in evangelism. He was not casual in his obedience to the heavenly vision; he was wholehearted, like Caleb. For you too, the Spirit's restraint may be part of His spiritual training, making you more responsive to His voice.

3. The Spirit may restrain you permanently because the step may not be God's will for you now or ever. It is never God's will for you to take a step that would bring disgrace. It is never His will for you to say unkind things. Ask yourself, is it true, kind, necessary? It is never His will for you to make a critical statement. It is never His will for you to question the sincerity of another until you know much about that person's inner life.

4. The Spirit may restrain you to keep you out of temptation. Christ taught us to pray, "Lead us not into temptation" (Matt. 6:13). God often answers this prayer by restraining us (Ps. 19:13).

5. The Spirit may restrain you to keep you out of danger. God sees all the contingencies of your life. He knows where you would meet careless drivers, where disease germs lurk, the plans of terrorists, criminals, and enemies of Christ, and all other dangers seen or unseen. I am alive today because of the restraint of the Spirit several times while I was in India; twice I was about to take a normally used street, but by God's restraint I escaped angry rioters.

While Dr. and Mrs. Dwight Ferguson were driving across Florida, he felt prompted to pull off onto the shoulder of the road. He felt a certain peace as he did so. The couple sat in the car until Dr. Ferguson felt free in spirit to resume driving. Five miles down the road they passed the site of a service station that had been blown away amid considerable damage in the area. A tornado had touched down right where they might have been had Dr. Ferguson not instantly obeyed the restraint of the Spirit.

6. The Spirit may restrain you to keep you from making statements by word or in writing that you would come to regret. You may think you understand, but you may lack many of the facts. Your best-intended remarks may do more harm than good, may wound instead of heal. The Holy Spirit will always restrain critical, sarcastic, or over-confident remarks or even well-intended but wrong suggestions if you are spiritually sensitive and responsive (Ps. 141:3).

7. The Spirit may restrain you from excessive levity that can dissipate the presence of the Lord and hinder God's blessing.

8. The Spirit may restrain you from overeating and the sin of gluttony against your body. He may restrain you from overworking or doing other things unwise for your health.

9. The Spirit may restrain your use of leisure time. He may check you from spending so much time with television, the newspaper, or comparatively unprofitable reading. All these innocent things may rob you of God's best—a more active and effective prayer life, a daily study of God's Word, time for visiting the sick, visiting the imprisoned, and witnessing to neighbors and friends. Many will be amazed in heaven at how many people were not won to Christ because they did not use their leisure time wisely.

10. The Spirit may restrain you from unwise financial steps. How many times have you made unwise financial expenditures because you did not pray enough or were insensitive to the restraints of the Spirit! How often would the Spirit like to restrain you in unwise steps in your employment or business! How often would He like to restrain you from trips during which He foresees that family emergencies will arise.

Nothing in life can be more practical and down to earth than the guidance and the restraint of the Spirit. He delights to help your planning and daily decisions. When you have developed a listening ear, it does not take a loud voice or a jolting event to guide you. It becomes natural to you to expect suggestions or restraints from the Spirit. Your life almost unconsciously becomes prayer without ceasing and guidance without ceasing.

"the mind of christ"
will guide you

We have the mind of Christ," said the apostle Paul (1 Cor. 2:16). What does Paul mean? He means you can understand scriptural truth as Christ did; you can share the wisdom of Christ. This wisdom, says Paul, has been planned by God for you even "before time began" (1 Cor. 2:7). It is vastly different from the thinking of the world. You become distinguished by having more Christlike thinking and a more Christlike lifestyle than unsaved persons.

Because the Holy Spirit enables you to view life, the world, relationships, and goals from Christ's perspective, you have a refreshingly different set of principles by which to make decisions. Instead of an earthly mind-set you have a spiritual mind-set aided by the Holy Spirit. Thus Paul refers to the "mind of the Spirit" (Rom. 8:27)—that is, the "mind of Christ."

"Your attitude," says Paul, "should be the same as that of Christ Jesus" (Phil. 2:5). The hymn writer expresses it:

> May the mind of Christ my Savior
> Live in me from day to day,
> By His love and power controlling
> All I do and say.   —*Katie Barclay Wilkinson*

The Holy Spirit so impresses on you the content of Scripture and the outlook of God that it is easy for Him to remind you to conform your thinking and living to Christ's perspective. You are enabled to be spiritually sensitive to what is Christlike.

This Christlike mind and attitude, Scripture based and Scripture guided, trains you "to distinguish good from evil" (Heb. 5:14), what pleases the Lord from what does not. It is an aspect of spiritual maturity to which Paul challenges us: "All of us who are mature should take such a view of things" (Phil. 3:15).

The world and its people have their own perspectives on life, their own patterns of priorities, attitudes, and lifestyles. Paul writes, "Do not conform any longer to the pattern of this world, but be transformed by the renewing of your mind. Then you will be able to test and approve what God's will is—his good, pleasing and perfect will" (Rom. 12:2). This is a beautiful description of how the mind of Christ guides you. The renewing of your mind comes by receiving more and more of the mind of Christ. This helps you test and choose as a way of life the things that please God. These are always what is "good," Paul says; they are the best for you.

Paul does not want you to live and act "like mere men" of the world (1 Cor. 3:3). That would make you "worldly," he says. Our age, our culture, our sin-dominated civilization seek to give us a worldly set of standards, desires, priorities, and attitudes. We are always in danger of the culture's penetrating and polluting our minds; almost before we know it, we can be pressed into its mold.

You need the constant, renewing ministry of the Spirit to remind you of the Christlike worldview, the Christlike counterculture. One day Christ will return and rule, and earth's culture will become a spiritual culture. Today Satan seeks to rob earth of the benefits of a culture that is good, pleasing, and perfect. So the Spirit today gives you the mind of Christ, the heaven-oriented mind, the eternity-oriented mind. To worldly minded people your basis of choice seems strange. But when they think seriously they must recognize that your Spirit-guided lifestyle is beautiful and right.

As a Spirit-filled believer you face the same set of circumstances and basic facts as others, but you are aided by a supernatural resource not available to the unsaved person. The Spirit has been forming in you the same attitudes that Christ has. You already have, to some degree, the mind of Christ and are developing ever more fully Christ's own perspective. You have a purer ethical frame of reference. Your value system has an eternal dimension. You have a resident, omniscient Counselor, the indwelling Holy Spirit. God's spiritual principles are written in your mind, on your heart.

> I will put my laws in their minds and write them on their hearts (Heb. 8:10, quoted from Jer. 31:33–34).

> I will give you a new heart and put a new spirit in you; I will remove from you your heart of stone and give you a heart of flesh. And I will put my Spirit in you and move you to follow my decrees and be careful to keep my laws (Ezek. 36:26–27).

This new inner heart attitude and motivation distinguishes you from the unsaved. You have "the mind of Christ." You have a new sensitivity to God.

Another biblical way to express this is that you as a Spirit-filled believer are now living "according to the Spirit" (Rom. 8:4). To live according to the Spirit is to be cleansed by the Spirit, guided by the Spirit, and empowered by the Spirit. Paul explains, "Those who live in accordance with the Spirit have their minds set on what the Spirit desires" (Rom. 8:5). He adds that this results in your sharing spiritual life and peace.

Therefore, to have the mind of Christ is to have Spirit-assisted understanding and wisdom that is in harmony with Christ. It is to have the perspective of Christ, to share the counsel of the Spirit, and to be motivated in accordance with the leading of the Spirit.

You have, says Paul, "put off your old self" (Eph. 4:22), which was motivated and hindered by sin's deceiving desires. You have been "made new in the attitude of your minds" (v. 23) and thus have "put on the new self" (v. 24). This new attitude of mind constantly influences your choices and decisions, even though you are often unaware of it.

As a Spirit-filled believer you have not only the truth of the Bible and the inner voice of the Spirit as primary resources for guidance, but also a Christlike perspective, an "according to the Spirit" frame of reference, and a new self. This truth has implications for all your daily living. You now have the mind of Christ.

how to develop "the mind of christ"

Having been encouraged by Paul to have the "mind of Christ," you are enabled to develop it through the ministry of the Holy Spirit.

1. Be constantly aware that Christ is with you, indwelling you by His Spirit. This brings all of life on a higher plane. This is not something you strive to achieve; this is spiritual fact. You are committed to Christ, He is now your Lord, and He has sovereign authority over you. He has committed Himself to you; you are covenanted together. You live for Him, with Him, and by His enabling. With Paul you can say, "For to me, to live is Christ" (Phil. 1:21). This now makes available to you the mind of Christ.

2. Constantly depend on the Holy Spirit. He cleanses, empowers, and fills you so that you now live "according to the Spirit" and not according to your sinful nature, as unsaved people do (Rom. 8:4–5). Your mind is now controlled by the Spirit (vv. 6–9).

As you live now on the spiritual plane, depend constantly on the Spirit, your ever-present Counselor, to alert you; to remind you; to suggest ideas, words, and actions; to motivate and encourage you; or to check and restrain you. Watch for His guidance in all your decisions. In life's thronging details, again and again and almost unconsciously glance to catch His smile or frown, His approval or His questioning of what you are doing or considering. As the ship's pilot keeps glancing at his compass and the stars to check his course, as the plane's pilot keeps looking at the dials of his instrument board, so keep lifting your spiritual eye to the Spirit and sense His continued approval, concern, or disapproval.

3. *Constantly desire to please God.* To have the mind of Christ is to share the attitude of Christ, who said, "The one who sent me is with me; he has not left me alone, for I always do what pleases him" (John 8:29).

> "My food . . . is to do the will of him who sent me and to finish his work" (John 4:34).
>
> "I seek not to please myself but him who sent me" (John 5:30).

Let this same motivation control you as you share the mind of Christ. More important to you than success, the praise of others, or your own wishes—more important than all else—must be your desire to please God, to sense His smile of approval and His loving pleasure in you.

4. *Constantly breathe the spirit of prayer and give priority to prayer.* Prayer was the very life-breath of Christ when He was on earth. He took whatever steps were necessary to find time and a place for prayer. He arose early in the morning to pray, prayed in the evening, and on occasion prayed all night. He went outside the village to be alone with God. He sent His disciples away so He could be alone in prayer. He climbed the mountain to find a secluded place to pray. But also, again and again wherever He was, He lifted His eyes and prayed. Prayer was as natural and as necessary to Christ as breathing.

Christ chose to live and minister during His incarnation, using the same methods and spiritual resources available to you and me. Normally as He ministered He derived His power by prayer, not by relying on His divine omnipotence. He prayed before He multiplied the loaves and fishes and before He raised Lazarus from the dead. He told Peter that Satan would try to sift him, but He would pray for him. Today He reigns sovereignly by intercession; His throne is an intercessory throne. He "lives to intercede" (Heb. 7:25). He is "at the right hand of God and is also interceding for us" (Rom. 8:34).

To have the mind of Christ is to put priority on prayer, to cover and saturate all you do by prayer, and to pray without ceasing.

To have the mind of Christ is to share His intercessory burden for the church and the world.

How do you fulfill your role of identifying with Christ by serving as "priests to serve our God" (Rev. 1:6; 5:10)? A vital part is receiving in prayer the constant flow of guidance as the Spirit brings prayer needs to your heart. Prayer is listening as well as speaking. It is through the listening ear during prayer that you identify with Christ in the prayer burdens for which He is interceding on His throne. Thus you are enabled constantly to do His will. Only through the mind of Christ can you properly represent Christ and mediate His blessing constantly to others.

5. *Constantly adopt and manifest the humility of Christ.* "Your attitude should be the same as that of Christ Jesus: Who . . . made himself nothing, taking the very nature of a servant. . . . he humbled himself and became obedient" (Phil. 2:5–8).

Let this humble servant attitude guide you, motivate you, and clothe you in all you say and do. Include it in the background of every decision you make. Constantly consider others better than yourself (Phil. 2:3). Let this attitude cover you like a beautiful garment in all you do and add graciousness to all you say (Col. 3:12).

The mind of Christ is not a passive mind—it is constantly seeking to obey God, live for God, and complete the tasks that God assigns. Your carnal self-nature must not protrude in all of this. Let the Christlike attitude of humility prevail. Be actively like Christ. Be totally committed to and dependent on God, and do all as to the Lord (1 Cor. 10:31; 1 Peter 4:1). Do all in the name of Christ (Col. 3:17).

6. *Constantly recognize and be motivated by the supreme worth of the spiritual.* Recognize that the spirit is more important than the body, and spiritual welfare than material welfare. "Man does not live on bread alone, but on every word that comes from the mouth of God" (Matt. 4:4). Jesus assures us that when we put spiritual interests first (His kingdom and His righteousness), all our material needs will be taken care of (Matt. 6:33). Christ makes no sharp dichotomy between the spiritual and the physical, but He always gives first place to the spiritual.

When you have the mind of Christ you will be looking for the spiritual potential or implications in everything you do. As you live your normal life in your very real world you will both consciously and unconsciously give priority to what is important spiritually. You remember, "What good is it for a man to gain the whole world, yet forfeit his soul?" (Mark 8:36). Why gain material, economic, or other success at the cost of the smiling approval of God?

7. *Constantly keep in view the perspective of eternity.* When you have the mind of Christ you are a person living in two worlds. You are a citizen of heaven as well as earth. You recognize how foolish it is to put most of your investments of time, effort, love, and finance in what may be lost at any time and will never last for more than a century. Rather, invest in what will result in eternal blessing, rewards, and joy.

As you make your countless decisions, remember that everything here is temporary, perishable, and capable of being quickly lost. But everything that is done for God, in the name of Jesus, and out of a desire to please the Lord, is an eternal investment. It is as sure to be rewarded as God is in heaven.

Paul said that all you do, your whole life, will be tested. Whatever is of the imperishable nature of gold, silver, and costly stones will survive the test of God's judging fire. But whatever is of the perishable nature of wood, hay, and straw will be burned up, and those parts of your life will be an eternal loss to you (1 Cor. 3:11–15). Since you have the mind of Christ, keep evaluating how you spend your time. Is it straw or gold?

The mind of Christ in you will help you to realize how much of your time spent in reading, in watching nonuplifting television, and in comparatively meaningless conversation will prove on the judgment day to have been as wood, hay, and straw. Realize that in many ways you can do your ordinary, daily work as unto the Lord. Use your spare moments in prayer, reading the Word, or in helping and blessing others. This, in the phrase of Dr. Stanley Tam, is transmuting your time and efforts into the gold of eternity. The mind of Christ can guide you in many of the seemingly trivial decisions of your daily life.

Paul says, "The spiritual man makes judgments about all things," and then adds, "We have the mind of Christ" (1 Cor. 2:15–16). The Greek word for "makes judgments" is *anakrinō* and expresses the questioning process that is basic to making a judgment. It involves inquiry and investigating in order to make decisions. In other words, the spiritual person does not just follow unquestioningly the standards or examples of others. He carefully inquires, observes, weighs evidence, and makes his decisions the way Christ would, for he has the mind of Christ.

Since you have Christ's attitude, set your heart on "things above, where Christ is seated at the right hand of God" (Col. 3:1). Set your mind "on things above, not on earthly things" (v. 2). Avoid putting excessive emphasis on what will make you wealthy or popular or what will give you a "good time." You do not despise money, for you know how necessary it is in life and how much good can be done with it. You know you can invest it for God. But money is not your priority.

You value the goodwill and good opinion of others. But you put all these in their proper place: subject to the will and glory of God. You enjoy relaxing alone or with family and friends. But you choose forms of relaxation that are physically, mentally, and spiritually beneficial. You try to avoid activities that largely waste time. Having the mind of Christ, try to find larger portions of your spare time and even your retirement time that you can use to make eternal investments.

8. *Constantly live and act in ways that keep your mind at peace in Christ.* Paul urges, "Let the peace of Christ rule in your hearts" (Col. 3:15). The Greek word *brabeuetō,* translated "rule," means literally to be an umpire, to arbitrate, to rule or to decide. Paul speaks in Colossians 3 of the areas where Christ's peace should be the umpire, the deciding authority—among the members of the body of Christ and in your own heart. Paul urges you to clothe yourself with compassion, kindness, humility, gentleness, and patience (v. 12). You are to bear with others and forgive whatever grievance you have against them (v. 13). You are to bind all these aspects of spiritual clothing around you with love (v. 14). That will prepare the way for Christ's peace to rule in your relations with others.

Then you are to be thankful (v. 15), feasting on God's Word and sharing its lessons with others as you gratefully sing and praise God (v. 16). Whatever you do or say, you are to do it thankfully in the name of Jesus (v. 17). It is in the middle of all these instructions that Paul urges you to let Christ's peace be your umpire. You will be very watchful of what deepens that peace or what begins to rob you of it. That blessed peace will guide you sweetly but firmly in what to do or not to do, what to say or not to say.

Peace! If any word or act will deepen your own heart peace and your peace with others, what more guidance do you need? If something robs you of peace, by all means avoid it. Guidance can be as simple as that. The mind of Christ will teach you to be a peace-maker, a peace-deepener, and a peace-maintainer. It will affirm to you, "This is the will of God, but that isn't." Then Isaiah 26:3 will be fulfilled in your life: "You will keep in perfect peace him whose mind is steadfast, because he trusts in you."

What can be more essential and practical when you have the Word of God and the indwelling Counselor, the Holy Spirit? What can be more important to cherish and to heed than the mind of Christ? The Bible, the voice of the Spirit, and the mind of Christ—these are the primary resources for your guidance. Use them.

30

PROVIDENCE CAN BE PERPLEXING

Now let us turn to the secondary sources of guidance.

God is always sovereignly active in His world. He governs with a fatherly care and in accord with both His overall plan for the world and His purpose for your life. Nothing ever touches you except as God wills it or permits it.

Nevertheless, because you are part of the human scene, many circumstances come into your life that are not directly the result of your own actions. You will not escape all problems and sorrows just because you are a Christian. But as a Christian you have God's special resources. You have God's special love and care. You have the guidance of the Spirit, the privilege of prayer, and the unseen ministry of angels to help in your circumstances or even at times to rearrange your circumstances.

In themselves, many events in your life seem problematical and even harmful. Most of life's circumstances may appear to have no special significance for your guidance. They are merely a part of life as God permits you to live it. But no circumstance is in total isolation. God surrounds the difficult circumstances with other circumstances and by His supervisory coordination causes things to work together for your good and His glory (Rom. 8:28).

Some events may be engineered by Satan to tempt you, mislead you, discourage you, or defeat you. To use such events as an indication of God's guidance is to fall into Satan's trap.

If Joseph had taken his being sold into slavery as an indication that he was out of God's will, he would have misread providence. If he had interpreted his imprisonment as an indication that God was indifferent to his faithfulness to purity, he could have failed God. God was using circumstances that in themselves were without adequate explanation in order to develop in Joseph character, maturity, and important personality traits. These prepared and qualified him to become one of the towering leaders of ancient history, a savior of both Israel and Egypt.

Joseph was God's man in God's place at God's time all the way from his teenage obedience to his father to his role as prime minister of Egypt at a time of international crisis. Joseph was able to look back and say, "You intended to harm me, but God intended it for good to accomplish what is now being done, the saving of many lives" (Gen. 50:20).

Physical, financial, or other forms of difficulty do not necessarily prove that God is displeased. Prosperity and the absence of difficulty do not necessarily indicate that God is blessing because you are in His will.

God does often make difficult the path of one outside His will. He may block the way in order to awaken the conscience or restrain from wrong steps. Balaam is an example of God's using difficulties to restrain. God explained to Balaam, "I have come here to oppose you because your path is a reckless one before me" (Num. 22:32). Solomon wrote, "The way of the unfaithful is hard" (Prov. 13:15).

Similarly, God often gives special blessing—spiritual, physical, or financial—as an indication of His approval. He repeatedly works circumstances together to make a smooth path for those fulfilling His will.

> The path of the righteous is level; O upright One, you make the way of the righteous smooth (Isa. 26:7).

> Along unfamiliar paths I will guide them; I will turn the darkness into light before them and make the rough places smooth. These are the things I will do; I will not forsake them (Isa. 42:16).

To summarize, life is filled with providences. Many of the circumstances of life are yours because you are part of the human scene. Some are perplexing; some are part of God's training for you. On the one hand, some are confirmatory of God's guidance to you or a part of His restraint; on the other hand, many have no special significance for your guidance. Some may even be traced to Satan's trying to discourage you, confuse you, and mislead you.

Providence in itself is not a safe guide. Providence is important, and God is in ultimate control of all providence. But providence is only one of the manifold elements that the Holy Spirit blends together and interweaves in the process of divine guidance. It is an important means of guidance, but providence is not your Guide. The Holy Spirit is your Guide, your abiding Counselor. The Holy Spirit guides concerning providence and through providence. But you need His illumination, His interpretation, and His seal and assurance.

providence helps
guide you

How does God use providential circumstances to help guide and to confirm His guidance to you. Let us see how God fits providences into His wonderful plan.

God is the sovereign of the whole universe. He is the Lord of history. He is at work in our circumstances. He has a great ultimate and eternal plan that He will never change. He planned for a beautiful world filled with a holy mankind in loving fellowship with Him and with one another. He planned to lavish His love eternally on mankind and planned for man to rule earth as His deputy.

Sin interrupted God's beautiful plan. Man's holiness and harmony were devastated, man's capacities and personality crippled, and the human race set off on a course of disobedience. Human history records man's constant misuse of his God-given and almost Godlike freedom. God provided Calvary so that man could repent and return to His fellowship.

God is permitting sinful man to explore to its logical end the total destructiveness of sin. History moves toward Armageddon and God's intervention by the return of Christ in power and glory. All God's original and ultimate plan will prevail. What was lost as recorded in the Book of Genesis will be restored as promised in the Book of Revelation. Sin and suffering will end. The curse will be lifted. God and man will live in eternal fellowship. There will be a new heaven and earth and a new Jerusalem.

How God Adjusts His Plan

God's sovereignty is so total, His wisdom so great, and His loving patience so amazing that He can accommodate great flexibility in His governing of the universe today without destroying His ultimate and eternal plan. He has built in provisions for the comparatively free actions of the animal creation, for man's exercise of the power of choice within the very wide limits set by God, and for Satan and his evil spirits' rebellious actions. But God also enforces strict limits for them (Job 1:12; 2:6).

Thus God constantly adjusts many details in the outworkings of His will in accordance with our choices. God sovereignly works in and coordinates all situations. He adjusts His actions to the repentance or rebellion of sinners and to the prayers and obedience of His children.

The Old Testament prophetic warnings were given to provide people and nations with an opportunity to repent and escape God's judgment that He had pronounced. Thus when David repented, God forgave and spared him the death penalty that he deserved (2 Sam. 12:1–14). He spared Nineveh when it repented at the preaching of Jonah, and God did not destroy it as He had announced He would do (Jonah 3).

This principle is clearly stated in Ezekiel 33:14–16:

> If I say to the wicked man, "You will surely die," but he then turns away from his sin and does what is just and right—if he gives back what he took in pledge for a loan, returns what he has stolen, follows the decrees that give life, and does no evil, he will surely live; he will not die. None of the sins he has committed will be remembered against him. He has done what is just and right; he will surely live.

God sovereignly overrules the actions of sinners. He overruled Pharaoh and the actions of Joseph's brothers (Gen. 50:20), and He even made pagan Cyrus (Isa. 44:28) and pagan Nebuchadnezzar (Jer. 25:9) His servants in some of their actions.

God normally permits storms, rain, drought, and other natural phenomena to follow what we call "the laws of nature"—laws He Himself ordained. But when it serves His purpose, God can overrule nature's laws by intervening in what we call "miracle power." This is only another example of His sovereign work. The laws of nature are descriptions of God's routine way of working; His intervention in miracles is His special working.

Because God is always in control of the universe and its laws, prayers can be answered, miracles can occur, and He can respond in mercy when men or nations turn to Him in repentance.

God works through His sovereign control of nature and His guiding and ultimate control of man so that a circumstance serves His purpose for His children. "And we know that in all things God works for the good of those who love him, who have been called according to his purpose" (Rom. 8:28).

Why You Must Interpret Circumstances With Caution

Because God normally permits nature to follow its laws, His creatures to use their power of choice within the limits He sets, and permits Satan and his deceiving spirits a surprising latitude of action, we can never assume that circumstances prove in themselves what is God's highest will. That was the mistake of Job's friends, and God had to rebuke their folly. They accused Job of being a great sinner because of his sufferings. Circumstances in themselves can be a very inadequate guide.

Nevertheless, God is in ultimate control and can coordinate even our free actions and fit them into His overall plan. He can and does set limits for Satan. He can and does intervene in supernatural ways; there are more of these miracle interventions in life than most people realize. God can and docs continually use providential circumstances to guide us.

God limits Satan and his demons and then overrules the evil they are permitted to do. He overrules the sins of the unsaved and the mistakes and failures of His children. Jesus said to Pilate, "You would have no power over me if it were not given to you from above" (John 19:11).

Because our minds are finite and because we cannot see the future, we are often perplexed as to why God does not limit Satan more, stop him sooner, or stop things from happening.

Because we are human, life will always hold mystery for us and we will be perplexed by insistent questions for which we have no adequate answers. God illuminates our problems with His presence, comforts us with His promises, and guides us through our decisions. But He may not remove us from the problems others cause us or the blessings they bring us. Guidance does not eliminate our taking up our cross to follow Jesus. To be guided by Christ will often lead to a cross. But it is the sure way to blessing.

Never make providential circumstances your primary source of guidance! Always seek additional confirmations from God that you are interpreting the circumstances correctly. The Holy Spirit will use Scripture, His inner voice in your heart, the mind of Christ that He is giving you, the remarks and advice of godly people, and other means to confirm to you what He permits circumstances to suggest. God is always ready to take additional reasonable steps to make His guidance certain if you are seeking His will and are still perplexed.

Sometimes providence may temporarily seem to contradict the guidance God has given you, but in God's perfect time every door into His plan will open before you. You do not need to take your own hands to force it open. Furthermore, God can close doors before you that He does not want you to enter. He is equally willing to use His key to open or close doors (Rev. 3:7).

God does not drive you; He leads you. "He calls his own sheep by name and leads them out. . . . He goes on ahead of them, and his sheep follow him because they know his voice" (John 10:3–4). If the Lord is leading, He will see that the doors open at the right time. The door opens for Him and you as you enter together. And remember: "See, I have placed before you an open door that no one can shut" (Rev. 3:8).

When God called Philip to leave the Samaria revival for a desert road, he had the hungry-hearted Ethiopian waiting. When God's angel awoke Peter and told him to follow, the prison gate was sure to open before him. God's call guarantees God's door. When Paul was guided by the call to Macedonia it was after God had called him, used him, and then blocked a series of possible doors. Then in the night God gave him a guidance bonus—a vision.

Neither did Paul accept an apparently closed door as meaning God was stopping him when he had other proofs that God had led him to that point. Though friends tried to stop him, prophecies warned of suffering ahead; and though he was mobbed, jailed, and delayed along the way, he pressed ahead to Jerusalem, knowing he was in the will of God. "Why are you weeping and breaking my heart?" Paul asked his well-meaning converts, the church leaders, and even his own evangelistic team members who were all pleading with him to stop. "I am ready not only to be bound, but also to die . . . for the name of the Lord Jesus" (Acts 21:13).

Amid all the sufferings and adversities that followed, the Lord continued to use Paul, stood by his side one night, and told him to take courage, adding, "You must also testify in Rome" (Acts 23:11). Again just before his shipwreck during the voyage to Rome, Paul could testify: "Last night an angel of the God whose I am and whom I serve stood beside me and said, 'Do not be afraid, Paul. You must stand trial before Caesar" (Acts 27:24). Paul added, "So keep up your courage, men, for I have faith in God that it will happen just as he told me" (v. 25).

It is possible to be so sure of God's guidance that nothing moves you. And if God sees that you need extra proofs of His good hand upon you and His full purpose for you, He is prepared to give you special assurances of His grace and power.

Your life's circumstances do not occur at random. When you are totally committed to God and constantly listening for His guiding voice, things don't "just happen" in your life. Events are not isolated happenings. God has a way of integrating them into His plan for His glory and for your eternal good. You are called according to God's purpose (see ch. 39). You love God. Therefore Romans 8:28 is your personal promise from the Lord.

Observe the circumstances about you. It will thrill you to see how God makes them fall into place as you stay true to His will. In themselves they are not enough to be sure of God's will. Wait on God till you have a deep inner assurance. The Holy Spirit is your Guide, not circumstances. But the Holy Spirit will see that all circumstances necessary for your obedience to God will work together for God's glory and His good plan for you. " 'I know the plans I have for you,' declares the Lord, 'plans to prosper you and not to harm you, plans to give you hope and a future'" (Jer. 29:11).

youR conscience helps GuiDe you

One of God's good gifts to man is conscience. It is a part of your personhood. The conscience is a God-enabled function of your being. You as a person have an inescapable conscience.

The Bible makes a clear distinction between your inner being (your "heart") and your conscience. You tend to recognize in your innermost being the morality and rightness of certain acts. Conscience "also" witnesses as you think about choices and actions. "They show that the requirements of the law are written on their hearts, their consciences also bearing witness, and their thoughts now accusing, now even defending them" (Rom. 2:15).

The same distinction is made in Titus 1:15: "Both their minds and consciences are corrupted." The conscience functions according to your values. It judges your thoughts, attitudes, words, and deeds. Your conscience uses your feelings to speak to you. When you realize something is wrong, your conscience reproves you. It is an instinctive capacity that has a threefold function:

1. Your conscience recognizes the difference between right and wrong.

2. Your conscience motivates you to do right and avoid wrong. For example, Paul says Christians should submit to government authorities "because of conscience" (Rom. 13:5).

3. Your conscience judges you. It gives you an inner sense of approval and peace when you do right. It condemns you and leaves you with guilt if you do wrong. As a result you experience inner distress, regret, and shame. You may even have remorse.

Thus your conscience is a witness to you from God. The Holy Spirit confirms and affirms your conscience. "I speak the truth in Christ . . . my conscience confirms it in the Holy Spirit" (Rom. 9:1). Paul could say, "Our conscience testifies that we have conducted ourselves in the world, and especially in our relations with you, in the holiness and sincerity that are from God" (2 Cor. 1:12).

Without conscience you could not be held accountable for your sin. The Greek word for "conscience" is *suneidēsis*, which literally means "a knowing with." It is co-knowledge. You know with God or with whatever you accept as your authority and standard (e.g., the Bible). God gives you conscience to be your special resource in making decisions. But it is a secondary resource, not a primary one, because it is always dependent on that which constitutes your standard and authority. If you are a Spirit-filled believer, it can depend on and agree with God, Scripture, your possession of the mind of Christ, and the Spirit's inner voice.

The extent to which your conscience is a safe guide depends on what it agrees with, or "co-knows." One's conscience is being trained from childhood as it accepts many of its values from the parents and home environment, school, and companions. It can develop biblically or secularly, wisely or unwisely, carefully or carelessly.

Conscience is born in you as a part of your inner nature, but its formation and training are gradual and lifelong. Your conscience makes moral choice possible, but it will reflect your values, whether they are right or wrong. It urges you to do what you believe to be right, but it does not make upright standards on its own.

The conscience of a person who is sanctified to the will of God and filled with the Holy Spirit will be a faithful guide to the extent that it is saturated with the Word of God and the mind of Christ and trained in mature spiritual discernment.

Your conscience might be compared to a computer. The computer makes calculations on the basis of the information fed into it. If incorrect data are fed into the computer, it will give incorrect answers. Similarly, if your conscience has received incorrect human opinions, misinterpretations of Scripture, or inadequate Bible teaching, it can mislead you. Your conscience may condemn you when it should not, or it may be silent when it ought to speak.

If you repeatedly disregard the voice of your conscience in some matter, its voice will become weaker and weaker until you do not even hear it speaking. Another way to describe this is to say that your conscience can become so accustomed or hardened by repeated failure to obey it that it becomes insensitive. Paul says a conscience can be seared as if by a hot iron (1 Tim. 4:2).

Biblical Descriptions of Conscience

Four times the Bible speaks of a "good conscience" (Acts 23:1; 1 Tim. 1:5, 19; 1 Peter 3:21). This is a conscience that has been properly taught and does not reprove you with a sense of guilt. Scripture also refers to a "clear conscience" seven times (Acts 24:16; 1 Cor. 4:4; 1 Tim. 3:9; 2 Tim. 1:3; Heb. 9:9; 13:18; 1 Peter 3:16). In one passage Paul speaks three times of a weak conscience (1 Cor. 8:7, 10, 12). This is one that has not been properly taught or trained. A guilty conscience is one that reproves a person for not living up to the standard that has been taught (Heb. 10:2, 22). A corrupted conscience (Titus 1:15) is one that has been taught wrong moral information and is no longer a reliable guide. A seared conscience (1 Tim. 4:2) is one that has become hardened by willful sin.

Thank God, a guilty or corrupted conscience can be cleansed by receiving through Christ's atonement the forgiveness of sins. Thus conscience, when scripturally taught, can serve a valuable role as your guide and can be used by the Holy Spirit (Rom. 9:1). It will witness to your doing God's will and will motivate you to preserve this clear witness (Rom. 13:5).

The conscience of a Christian takes one of four forms, according to the Bible.

The weak conscience. Paul speaks of the weak conscience in 1 Corinthians 8:7–12. It is the conscience of a Christian who is inadequately informed about the Word of God and the will of God. You may try very carefully to live up to your conscience legalistically, yet become convicted by it for doing something that is not biblically wrong. A weak conscience is a conscience in bondage to man's traditions, to other people's opinions, and sometimes to Satan's accusations. It is not a safe guide.

The careless conscience. The opposite of the weak conscience is the careless conscience. This person is not sufficiently conscientious. He is so casual in his obedience to Christ and so accepting of almost any conduct or belief that he lowers biblical standards of conduct to a level unacceptable to God. It is not a safe guide.

The good conscience. Paul testified to the Sanhedrin, "I have fulfilled my duty to God in all good conscience to this day" (Acts 23:1). His exhortation to Timothy was, "Fight the good fight, holding on to faith and a good conscience" (1 Tim. 1:18). A good conscience implies, says Paul, the conscientious fulfillment of Christian duty (Acts 23:1). At the new birth our sins are forgiven and our conscience cleansed by the blood of Christ (Heb. 9:14). In the full surrender that leads to the sanctifying infilling of the Holy Spirit, there is always a new and deeper commitment to the will of God.

The goal of God for each believer is Christian maturity (1 Tim. 1:5) that is built on (a) a pure heart, which you receive by faith when you make your total surrender to God and trust Him for the infilling of His Spirit (Acts 15:8–9; Phil. 3:15; 1 Peter 1:22), and (b) a good conscience, constantly guiding and motivating you in your Christian life (1 Tim. 1:5–6). Then as you war your spiritual warfare you can be constantly victorious (1 Tim. 1:18–19) by holding on to your faith and a good conscience.

The clear conscience. The confident and victorious testimony of Paul was, "I strive always to keep my conscience clear before God and man" (Acts 24:16). He not only wanted to live a life that would testify to Christ and glorify Christ, but he wanted to keep blameless in the light of his own conscience before both God and man. "I thank God, whom I serve . . . with a clear conscience" (2 Tim. 1:3). He urged the deacons, "Keep hold of the deep truths of the faith with a clear conscience" (1 Tim. 3:9). Thus your conscience should testify clearly to two things: your doctrine and your conduct.

The consciences of the unsaved are described by three terms in the Bible.

The guilty conscience. Hebrews 10:2 speaks of feeling guilty for sins committed (the Greek uses the word for "conscience"). It is normal for sinners to feel guilty for their sins. In this New Testament dispensation, the Holy Spirit convicts us of our guilt (John 16:8) and, when we repent and confess our sin and trust in Christ for forgiveness, the Holy Spirit gives us the blessed inner testimony to our forgiveness and salvation. This is called "the witness of the Spirit" (Rom. 8:16; 2 Cor. 1:22; Eph. 1:13). The Spirit bears testimony within us because the blood of Christ cleanses our conscience (Heb. 9:14).

The corrupted conscience. Paul teaches that corrupted people who do not believe cannot make proper moral judgments and decisions. "In fact, both their minds and consciences are corrupted" (Titus 1:15). Jesus said, "If then the light within you is darkness, how great is that darkness!" (Matt. 6:23). The corrupted conscience leads one deeper and deeper into moral darkness and perversity.

The seared conscience. The ultimate in an evil conscience in scriptural terms is the seared conscience. This refers to a person whose conscience has become so corrupted that he deliberately teaches people to believe what he knows to be error and to do what he knows to be sin (1 Tim. 4:2).

Let us turn from this dark picture.

How can we as Christians train our conscience so that we will never be misled? How can we train it to serve as our secondary but very important resource in divine guidance?

Conscience, I repeat, is only as safe a guide as its source of authority and the training given to it. Habitually obeyed, it speaks with awesome authority in your soul. Ultimately God and His Word are the only safe authority for your conscience. Paul testified, "My conscience is clear, but that does not make me innocent. It is the Lord who judges me" (1 Cor. 4:4).

you can train your conscience

)

Conscience is not static. It can grow stronger or weaker. It is constantly learning and being shaped by the influences upon it.

If your background has been very permissive, it may be that today your conscience allows you to do many things that are not best for you spiritually and are not in harmony with God's highest will for you. However, if you have previously had a very restrictive background, your conscience may bother you about many things that are not in conflict with God's will. You feel a psychological guilt, not a spiritual guilt, when you do them. Your conscience was taught a human tradition, not full, biblical liberty. The Spirit longs to take you from where you are today and give you a wholesome, Bible-guided, mature conscience.

What an opportunity for us as Christians! Paul said, "So I strive always to keep my conscience clear before God and man" (Acts 24:16). "Strive" is the translation of a Greek word that means to endeavor, to take pains, to exercise by training, to discipline.[1] This suggests the disciplined endeavor of an athlete who spends time and strength to train. It points to constant, habitual practice done in a methodical way.

Another Greek word used by Paul and the writer to the

---

[1] W. E. Vine, *The Expanded Vine's Dictionary of New Testament Words* (Minneapolis: Bethany House, 1984), p. 389.

Hebrews is *gumnazō,* from which we derive our word *gymnasium.* It also suggests diligent, strenuous, disciplined training. Paul exhorts Timothy, "Train [*gumnazō*] yourself to be godly" (1 Tim. 4:7).

No discipline [*paideia*—the training, discipline, and correction of a child] seems pleasant at the time, but painful. Later on, however, it produces a harvest of righteousness and peace for those who have been trained [*gumnazō*] by it (Heb. 12:11).

Solid food is for the mature, who by constant use have trained [*gumnazō*] themselves to distinguish good from evil (Heb. 5:14).

How do you do this disciplined, strenuous training?

Set Standards for Your Conscience

1. Recognize which standards are Bible-based or God-given. These should be held to unswervingly.

2. Recognize the various forms of Bible truth.

    a. Clear-cut statements of the Bible that are not modified by other statements.

    b. Bible statements that must be seen in their context to be properly understood. This includes the cultural situation existing at the time that part of Scripture was written.

    c. Bible statements that must be harmonized with other scriptural statements on the same subject. Whenever a subject is touched on in more than one Scripture passage, these must be compared and synthesized.

    d. Bible truth that is not based on simple, clear-cut statements but instead is derived from the whole pattern of Scripture teaching. Study everything in Scripture that has any relation to the issue you are considering. Then harmonize and synthesize this into a clear summary that you can express in words and write down. Examples: the use of tobacco and harmful drugs; the evil of abortion.

    e. Bible teaching may have general implications for the issue you are considering, but may have nothing specific or no real parallel. Here you must ask God's special guidance, seek to act in the general light of Scripture, or respond as you believe Jesus would. Avoid being dogmatic as if you have the only possible view. Examples: the Christian's duty as a citizen; how to keep the Lord's Day sacred.

3. *Recognize that on some passages of Scripture, godly teachers and leaders have wide disagreement.* If the matter that concerns you were an all-essential standard for conduct, God would undoubtedly have made Scripture more explicit. Accept the interpretation that most commends itself to your heart, but avoid dogmatism. Recognize that other interpretations may be valid. Remember Romans 14:5: "Each one should be fully convinced in his own mind."

4. *Make Christ your model and example.* Jesus said, "Whoever serves me must follow me" (John 12:26). Peter said that Christ left His example concerning how to endure suffering, "that you should follow in his steps" (1 Peter 2:21). Jesus said in reference to humility, "Learn from me" (Matt. 11:29). As He washed His disciples' feet, Jesus said, "I have set you an example that you should do as I have done for you" (John 13:15). Ask yourself, what would Jesus do if He were here?

5. *Receive guidance from the mind of Christ that the Spirit is forming in you.* These attitudes will help set your standards.

6. *Form your standards in the light of the lives of godly Christians.* Weigh the lives of others in the light of Scripture and the mind of Christ. You cannot make anyone your example in everything. Neither dare you make someone else's conscience your guide indiscriminately. Yet the Bible does point to the value of following godly examples. Some lives are a real message: "You show that you are a letter from Christ . . . written not with ink but with the Spirit of the living God" (2 Cor. 3:3).

> Imitate those who through faith and patience inherit what has been promised (Heb. 6:12).

> Remember your leaders, who spoke the word of God to you. Consider the outcome of their way of life and imitate their faith (Heb. 13:7).

Paul explains, "You yourselves know how you ought to follow our example" (2 Thess. 3:7), adding, "We did this . . . in order to make ourselves a model for you to follow" (v. 9).

Paul also wrote, "I urge you to imitate me" (1 Cor. 4:16). However, he added this safeguard in the same letter: "Follow my example, as I follow the example of Christ" (11:1).

7. *Don't try to get all other Christians always to see the same light*

you do. Paul wrote on one occasion, "Whatever you believe about these things keep between yourself and God" (Rom. 14:22). In other words, don't be judgmental of others. "Accept him whose faith is weak, without passing judgment on disputable matters. . . . Who are you to judge someone else's servant? To his own master he stands or falls" (Rom. 14:1–4).

Train Your Conscience

1. Thank God for your conscience. You depend on it even though much of the time you are almost unconscious of it.

2. Ask God to keep your conscience tender and alert.

3. Ask God to guide you in gathering the input your conscience needs. Seek and welcome all the facts. Don't avoid facts that disagree with your preliminary conclusion or your own bias.

4. Respect your conscience. When it begins to feel uneasy, pause prayerfully and ask God to show you if you have disobeyed or misunderstood, or are about to make a wrong decision. If you have not disobeyed, perhaps your conscience is questioning because it has inadequate or wrong training.

5. Confess to God repeatedly your total dependence on Him to enlighten and strengthen your conscience.

6. Be willing to accept new standards for your conscience for biblical reasons, as you understand Bible truths better.

7. Live in God's Word. The more you read, meditate, and study the Bible, the better equipped is your conscience to guide you.

8. Develop the mind of Christ as the Spirit assists you. Keep filled with the Spirit and seek to bear His fruit (Gal. 5:22–23).

9. Don't be hasty in making up your mind when you are faced with a new moral decision which seems confusing. Be willing to take time in searching for God's will.

> It is not good to have zeal without knowledge, nor to be hasty and miss the way (Prov. 19:2).

> Do you see a man who speaks in haste? There is more hope for a fool than for him (Prov. 29:20).

> My dear brothers, take note of this: Everyone should be quick to listen, slow to speak (James 1:19).

If you call out for insight and cry aloud for understanding, and if you look for it as for silver and search for it as for hidden treasure, then you will understand the fear of the LORD and find the knowledge of God (Prov. 2:3–5).

10. Welcome new light on any issue or standard, and especially if it is given from godly sources. You have not reached perfection yet. Be willing to accept advice.

Listen to advice and accept instruction, and in the end you will be wise (Prov. 19:20).

Make plans by seeking advice (Prov. 20:18).

Apply your heart to instruction and your ears to words of knowledge (Prov. 23:12).

11. When you are convinced of the rightness of a standard your conscience has adopted, make no exceptions unless God gives you adequate new light.

Guidelines for Your Conscience

1. Do everything for God's glory. When this is your supreme motive, it helps you evaluate many situations and gives strong training to your conscience (1 Cor. 10:31). Another way to say this is to do everything as you believe Jesus would. He always lived for the glory of the Father.

2. Do not sacrifice your conscience for anyone or anything. "Above all else, guard your heart, for it is the wellspring of life" (Prov. 4:23). Remember that from your pure heart and conscience will flow rivers of blessing and beams of light to others.

3. Depend on the Spirit to give special illumination in urgent moments of crisis. If you live faithfully in the fullness of the Spirit, He will not fail you when you need Him.

4. Let nothing enslave or master you. " 'Everything is permissible for me'—but not everything is beneficial. 'Everything is permissible for me'—but I will not be mastered by anything" (1 Cor. 6:12). Paul resolved not to let even an innocent habit master him. Just because a habit is not mentioned in Scripture does not make it right or wise.

5. *Avoid doubtful acts on which your conscience is not clear.* Paul gives a good example of this in the matter of diet (Rom. 14:23).

6. *Do nothing with the praise of men as your primary motive.* "We are not trying to please men but God, who tests our hearts. . . . We were not looking for praise from men, not from you or anyone else" (1 Thess. 2:4–6).

34

USE COMMON SENSE AND WISDOM

Common sense is another of God's great gifts to you. You depend on it constantly in the normal choices of your daily living.

Common sense in itself is not an adequate source of guidance. It is a secondary resource. No one has perfect common sense. Some are more lacking than others. This may result from inexperience, lack of careful observation, strong personal prejudice, or never having mastered logical thinking. But though inadequate as an independent guide, it is always God's gift to you to help you in the process of guidance.

God has created you with a mind that gathers facts, thinks through the meaning of these facts, and then chooses your course of action. You make sound judgments through your common sense. This ability to observe, think, and decide is a part of your personhood; it increases through training and experience.

As a Christian you can ask for the help of the Holy Spirit to assist you in observing more accurately, thinking more clearly, and deciding more wisely. The general term is "common sense." Because we Christians constantly depend on the Holy Spirit, we term it "sanctified common sense." Jauncy says, "Guidance is highly concentrated and sanctified thinking."[1]

---

[1] Quoted in Lloyd John Ogilvie, *Discovering God's Will in Your Life* (Eugene, Oreg.: Harvest House, 1982), p. 57.

When you pray for the Spirit's aid in your common sense, be sure that you do your part. "Do not be foolish [literally, "without mind, reckless in use of your mind"], but understand what the Lord's will is" (Eph. 5:17). You are responsible to use your mind, to develop the capacity to reason clearly. Don't rely on feelings to make decisions.

The Spirit does not do your work for you. He assists when you do your part. You must be careful as well as prayerful and use self-discipline—then the Spirit will do His special enabling.

Common Sense in Normal Daily Living

Common sense at its highest levels of sound judgment merges into wisdom. As a Christian you desire common sense and wisdom to bring glory to God. You remember God's promise, and when you face an important decision you take a moment to ask God for wisdom and guidance.

If you recognize a weakness in your process of making decisions, in your common sense, discipline yourself to be more careful and prayerful. What prejudices or biases do you need to guard against? Do you tend to jump to conclusions before you have gathered all the facts? Do you procrastinate or avoid decisions? Request a Christian friend to point out when you fall back into one of these weaknesses.

Ask for Wisdom

The Bible has much to say about wisdom, the highest level of common sense. It is sanctified common sense transformed by the anointing and guidance of the Spirit into true wisdom.

Christ promised to give words and wisdom (Luke 21:15). God gave wisdom to Stephen (Acts 6:10); even unsaved people recognized this. God gave Joseph wisdom in his role in Egypt (Acts 7:10). He gladly lavishes wisdom and understanding on us (Eph. 1:8; Col. 1:9). He desires that our relations with others be marked by wisdom and making the most of every opportunity (Col. 4:5).

By your conscious effort bring Christ into your daily thinking, reasoning, and deciding. "Trust in the LORD with all your heart and lean not on your own understanding; in all your ways acknowledge him, and he will make your paths straight [alternate translation: 'he will direct your paths']" (Prov. 3:5–6).

As you do this, Christ becomes your "wisdom from God" (1 Cor. 1:30). Gift and Giver are one. But this is not automatic. It is as you ask Him and acknowledge Him in all you do that He expresses His wisdom through your thinking.

His wisdom flows through your mind, makes use of the facts you have carefully gathered, helps you think clearly and deeply, and adds His depth of perception and insight. It becomes His anointing on your understanding, an anointing that "teaches you about all things" (1 John 2:27). You submit and consecrate your best thinking to Him. He by His Spirit makes you more alert, more perceptive, and wiser than you are in yourself.

Solomon, the wisest person who ever lived, knew his own wisdom was inadequate. So he made wisdom his priority request from God (1 Kings 3:5–14). His desire so pleased the Lord that He gave Solomon a "wise and discerning heart." It pleases God when you ask Him each day for wisdom in all you do. Then you bring the most glory to God. He truly becomes your wisdom.

If you feel your lack of this sanctified, Spirit-anointed common sense, or wisdom, ask of God. He will give to you generously without finding fault (James 1:5).

Normally the step indicated by your sanctified common sense is God's will for you. If God's will contradicts your common sense, He will give you clear guidance and confirmation. The dramatic occasions when God guides you to do something your sanctified mind would not expect are very few. But God, your Father, will not leave you in the dark about any unusual step that He requires you to take.

The Spirit sent Philip away from the revival in Samaria, where God was using him for the salvation of multitudes, and put him on a desert road sixty-five miles away. That was not the common sense thing to do. So God made the instruction perfectly clear to Philip. Then He confirmed it both by bringing the salvation of the Ethiopian eunuch and by physically catching Philip away (Acts 8).

When God sent Peter to the Gentile Cornelius, it was not the common sense thing for a Jew to do. So God made it especially clear by repeating a special vision three times. He confirmed this by causing the messengers Cornelius had sent to arrive at that exact time. He further confirmed it by pouring out the Spirit on Cornelius and his house when Peter arrived at Caesarea (Acts 10).

But normally the step that is correct according to your sanctified common sense is God's will for you. Let us consider several practical situations to illustrate this principle.

Example 1. Medical science has established that the use of tobacco is harmful to your health, makes you more susceptible to cancer, and can shorten your life. The Bible teaches that your body is a temple of the Holy Spirit:

> Don't you know that you yourselves are God's temple and that God's Spirit lives in you? If anyone destroys God's temple, God will destroy him; for God's temple is sacred, and you are that temple (1 Cor. 3:16–17).

> Do you not know that your body is a temple of the Holy Spirit, who is in you, whom you have received from God? You are not your own; you were bought at a price. Therefore honor God with your body (1 Cor. 6:19).

Sanctified common sense tells you that it is the will of God that you not use tobacco in any form. You do not need to pray and seek God's guidance. His will is already clear through Scripture, the facts of medical science, sanctified common sense, and probably the gentle voice of the Spirit in your heart. To use tobacco is to do that which is not God's best for you. It is to yield to temptation.

If you need God's special miracle help to overcome the craving of this habit, you have every right to pray and ask God for the Spirit's enabling. He desires to help you do the will of God.

Example 2. Many Christians are overweight. It is a medical fact that this tends to shorten life expectancy and makes one more liable to several serious diseases. If you are overweight, the same Scriptures cited in the first example apply to you. You are not your own; you owe the Lord as long a life as you can give Him.

Therefore God expects you to use self-discipline in diet and in exercise to bring your weight under control. To overeat is usually proof that you are a slave to your appetite, and God wants you to be free. You need not take time to seek God's will in this matter; sanctified common sense tells you it is time to do something.

There are some people who by heredity or from overeating in childhood tend to be overweight. If there are special medical facts involved, the doctor's advice is part of God's gift to you. Use it. But even in that case, ask the Spirit's special help in self-discipline in your regular habits of snacking, eating, and exercising. He desires to help you control your weight. But you must do your part in self-discipline.

Example 3. You and your family would like to make a special expenditure. You would all enjoy it, but you do not absolutely need it, and you do not have the cash on hand. Perhaps you are considering a late model car, a new television set, or a vacation trip. The general facts in the case are these:

—Interest rates are high and in the long run will greatly increase the cost.
—This item is not absolutely essential to your health or vocation.
—The Scripture fact is: "Let no debt remain outstanding, except the continuing debt to love one another" (Rom. 13:8).

Sanctified common sense then tells you to wait until you have the cash on hand. You do not need to ask God's guidance in this matter.

Perhaps God will use this delay to help train you in regular saving and planning ahead so that you will normally have money on hand for whatever you need. (Incidentally, in the light of spiritual needs, the need of world evangelization, and world hunger, you would get greater reward in heaven if you lived more simply and invested more of your finance for eternity.)

Many have changed from the habit of credit purchasing to saving in advance, anticipating needs, and paying cash. They praise the Lord that He led them to make this biblical change. Dr. Stanley Tam, president of U.S. Plastics, is a strong witness to this. His messages on transmuting your labor and money into the gold of eternity—the salvation of souls—have blessed many.

Common Sense in Special Decisions

In the ordinary details of life, your sanctified common sense will work almost unconsciously much of the time. Discipline yourself to check through the following steps until they become a part of your normal approach to life. When special crises come, make very prayerful and deliberate use of these steps.

1. *Observe all details carefully.* Be careful that you do not overlook anything. Don't expect God to bless your carelessness. Close observation of details is part of your responsibility in guidance. You may need to list all the details so that you can review them. List the pros and the cons of the decision.

2. *Free yourself from all ideas, emotions, and attitudes that might influence your observation and thinking.* Be careful not to be unduly influenced by others. Ask God to help you be truly free from all pressures and make the most prudent decision. If you are emotionally involved or have strong feelings pro or con, you may make a wrong decision without realizing it. Be as neutral as you can to everything except the will of God. That takes priority over all else, regardless of how it affects you personally.

3. *Seek to understand all the facts.* Check that you have not overlooked anything. Be careful not to draw premature conclusions. Trust God to help you see the situation as He sees it.

4. *Be willing to consult or receive advice from other people.* The common sense of others may be needed to balance yours, or to serve as a double check. Do not be too proud to take the counsel of specialists. Place special value on the words of those who are unbiased but mature in judgment and experience.

5. *Above all else, submit your common sense to any light from your primary resources in guidance.*

    a. Is there anything in God's Word that shines light on this situation?

    b. Is the Holy Spirit's inner voice suggesting any response on your part or step which you should take? Is He causing you to feel hesitant, or is He restraining you in any way?

    c. Is there any light from your having "the mind of Christ"? Is there a basic Christian perspective that you should take into consideration?

6. *Make your decision when you need to do so.* Do not fear; having taken steps as suggested above in dependence on the Spirit, act

according to your sanctified common sense. God will show you if you are making a mistake (Isa. 30:21).

Paul and his team provide an example. Paul's desire and sanctified common sense made him plan to evangelize in the Roman province of Asia, but the Holy Spirit restrained the group by some deep inner impression. They started toward Bithynia and again felt the Spirit restraining. They started in a third direction to Troas, and that night God gave Paul the Macedonian vision (Acts 16:6–10).

The team "got ready at once to leave for Macedonia, concluding that God had called" them to evangelize there. *Concluding* is a translation of a Greek word meaning "to put separate facts together in the mind." What facts?

    a. Paul was still called to evangelize.
    b. The first two alternatives were not God's will.
    c. Now a vision pointed to "Macedonia."

So by a combination of God's restraining, human reasoning, and a special "divine guidance," the group became sure of God's call.

7. *Watch for God to confirm your decision* by His providence, by comments of other Christians or mature people, and by inner peace, assurance, and joy.

35

GOD MAY GUIDE YOU THROUGH OTHERS

One reason why the Holy Spirit at the moment of your new birth baptizes you into the body of Christ (1 Cor. 12:13) is that you need the fellowship, mutual ministry, counsel, and leadership of other believers. We need one another far more than many Christians realize. We never outgrow the need for the prayer, the love, the acceptance, and the ministry of others.

You are not self-sufficient. Fellowship is essential to your sanity, health, and joy. For adequate spiritual growth, for wise spiritual ministry to the unsaved, and for the most wholesome investment of your life, you need other Spirit-filled believers.

The younger you are in the faith or the more inexperienced you are in any ministry into which God leads you, the more you need the fellowship and counsel of godly, mature, experienced Christians. God gives the church pastors and leaders because we need them. There is a spirit of independence in our age that runs contrary to the Bible. The body of believers is not always right, and your spiritual leader may not always be right. But you should have very good reasons if you disregard their counsel.

Wise, godly counsel is needed today more than ever before. We live in an age of unusual pressures. The complicated interpersonal relationships in work and society, the mobility of the population, and the competitiveness in all of life all conspire to make us need counsel. The breakdown of the home, psychological problems, and mental illness have added to life's pressures and complexities. We seem to be prone to confusion, problems, and inadequacies.

Society has developed an urgent need of educational counselors, financial counselors, family counselors, employment counselors, management counselors, psychiatric counselors, and a host of other highly specialized counselors. We all admit that no one knows it all. It is folly to try to do everything yourself.

To the Christian, the need of wise and frequent advice, informed counsel, and the recognition of interdependence is nothing new. Scripture reveals God as your primary Counselor. Scripture promises the guidance you need. The Bible has many examples of both wise and unwise counsel. The Book of Proverbs places much emphasis on advice. Paul outlines God's plan for mutual interdependence and mutual spiritual ministry to one another in the body of Christ (Rom. 12:4–5; 1 Cor. 12:14–26).

Every Christian is to be willing to give and receive counsel. No one has all the wisdom; no one is infallible. In Ephesians 5:22 Paul tells the wives to submit to the husbands, but in the preceding verse he includes the husbands' being submissive to the wives; he says, "Submit to one another out of reverence for Christ." Christian leadership has authority, but it must always be exercised in a doubly submissive way—to one another and to Christ.

Basic Principles of Counsel by Others

1. Ultimately all decisions are your personal responsibility. God made you in His image so you can make wise decisions. You are not to submit the final authority of life to anyone but God.

2. God is your primary Counselor. Scripture is your final authority. God counsels primarily through Scripture and the Spirit's inner voice. You should go to Him for counsel more often than you go to any human being. In all major decisions go to Him before you go to man.

3. Never make anyone's counsel a substitute for divine guidance. No pastor, religious leader, fellowship group, local church, discipleship group, or denomination has the right to claim your absolute obedience. Church standards are legitimate if they are supported by Scripture. But if God convinces you that your church is wrongly interpreting and applying Scripture, the church cannot on that point be your conscience. No discipleship group can be your conscience. Absolutely no one has a right to be your judge, your god. It is to God alone you must ultimately give account. You will one day stand before Him, and so will all other believers, regardless of their spirituality, leadership role, or spiritual prominence.

If church requirements on relatively minor matters cannot be found in the Bible, you may choose to follow them for the sake of fellowship, unity, and ministry. But no one should demand your unquestioning obedience. Don't sell your soul to anyone. Don't sell your usefulness to God and your Christian effectiveness for the sake of conformity.

There are two dangerous extremes. First, it is dangerous to be so independent that you rarely accept counsel, do not wholeheartedly accept the leadership of others, and cannot find any spiritual group with which you are comfortable. Submit to the wise and godly leadership of others. You are not a pope. Second, it is dangerous to accept any other person or group as your constant authority. You must not make any church, group, or person your pope.

John Robinson, pastor of the refugee Puritans in Leiden, gave wise counsel when he bade farewell to the Pilgrims embarking on the Mayflower. He said, "I charge you, that you follow me no farther than you have seen me follow the Lord Jesus Christ. The Lord has more truth to break forth out of His Holy Word."[1]

4. *Give special consideration to the counsel of those who have authority over you.* The Bible teaches submission of children to their parents (Eph. 6:1; Col. 3:20), wives to husbands (Eph. 5:22–24; Col. 3:18), younger adults to older ones (1 Peter 5:5), employees to employers (Eph. 6:5–8; Col. 3:22–24), and church members to church leaders (1 Thess. 5:12–13; Heb. 13:17).

But there is also biblical instruction on how those in authority are to exercise their authority. Husbands are to treat their wives considerately as partners and co-heirs of God (1 Peter 3:7) and to love them as much as they love themselves (Eph. 5:25, 33). Parents are not to discourage or embitter the children (Col. 3:21).

---

[1] Quoted in Andrew Murray, *The Spirit of Christ* (Minneapolis: Bethany Fellowship, 1979), p. 265.

Employers are to be right and fair (Col. 4:1) and not threaten or show favoritism (Eph. 6:9). Church leaders are to serve, be an example, and not "lord it over" others (1 Peter 5:2–3).

Though there is need of proper leadership and authority in life, the Bible also teaches that those in authority must be submissive to those under their supervision (Eph. 5:21). Christ has no room for mini-lords in His church. All counsel and command are to be given Christianly, without discouraging, embittering, or threatening.

No Christian has a right to demand that you accept his counsel just because he has authority. Scripture does say, "Obey your leaders and submit to their authority" (Heb. 13:17); but the word translated "obey" is a Greek word meaning "to be persuaded or won over." The obedience taught is "not by submission to authority, but results from persuasion."[2] The word *submit* here is described by Vaughn: "It seems to express that yielding of the self-will to the judgment of another, which recognizes constituted authority even while it retains personal independence."[3]

The Bible gives the person under authority liberty to raise questions. The Psalmist often questioned God; Job did, the prophets did, and even Jesus did in Gethsemane. It need not be disrespectful to ask a question or a reason. No one of age and in a right mind has the obligation to accept counsel without question just because an authority figure says it. Even God says to the sinner, "Come now, let us reason together" (Isa. 1:18) and "Review the past for me, let us argue the matter together" (Isa. 43:26).

5. When there is contradiction between any person's counsel and God, obey God. We naturally give great weight to counsel of our family, but God must always have priority. Jesus did not act just because His mother spoke (John 2:5), because His family desired it (Mark 3:31–35), or because His close friends asked Him (John 11:6).

When you turn to man more than to God, you will become confused and will hear less clearly the Spirit's inner voice. "Cursed is the one who trusts in man, who depends on flesh for his strength

---

[2] Vine, *An Expository Dictionary,* p. 796.

[3] H. Orton Wiley, *The Epistle to the Hebrews* (Kansas City, Mo.: Beacon Hill Press, 1959), p. 426.

and whose heart turns away from the LORD" (Jer. 17:5). At times God may lead you contrary to the advice of your best friends and thus teach you to rely even more on Him.

Ahaziah brought spiritual downfall and death on himself and tragedy to the nation because he followed the counsel of his mother and in-laws. They were not spiritually competent to guide him (2 Chron. 22:2–9). You too can make a tragic mistake if you follow someone's unwise advice.

For a discussion of conflict of authority in the case where the authority person is a non-Christian, see appendix C.

6. *No one's counsel is to be accepted just because that person counseled you correctly in the past.* No person has all the answers or is always right. Every person, no matter how godly, is biased in some areas, inadequately informed in many, and liable to mistake. Do not idolize any counselor. The more you respect the person, the more watchful you need to be to evaluate his counsel. Just because a person is an authority in one area does not necessarily mean he is an authority in the area in which you need advice. When you ask for advice, be sure to ask what your friend understands to be the teaching of God's Word and what is most in harmony with the mind of Christ in the matter. Don't just ask for an opinion. Ask for the facts and reasons.

7. *Use the counsel of others after you sense guidance.* After you feel you have received the Spirit's guidance is the best time to seek the wise, confirming counsel of carefully chosen confidants. Or, if you have kept a matter before the Lord for some time and see two or more possible courses of action, you may ask counsel in the effort to get additional information or perspective. Sometimes God will use one of His children who knows nothing about your need of guidance to say something that will confirm the guidance God has given. This is probably what happened in Acts 13:2 when the Spirit said, "Set apart for me Barnabas and Saul for the work to which I have called them." Apparently God had already spoken to Barnabas and Saul.

8. *In major decisions use several counselors.* "Plans fail for lack of counsel, but with many advisers they succeed" (Prov. 15:22). Compare Proverbs 11:14; 20:18; and 24:6. David had two special advisers; he did not depend on one alone. However, to make many

advisers one's primary source of guidance can lead to confusion. Don't just consult with people who are likely to agree with you.

9. *Majority opinions must be seriously considered but may not be correct.* There is obviously great weight when a large number of counselors agree, but they can all be wrong. Ahab followed the majority advice and was killed (1 Kings 22). Sometimes one person, such as Micaiah, who prophesied against Ahab, is in the right and guided by the Lord, while the majority are wrong.

10. *Give greater attention to the advice of Christians.* While some Christians may be immature, unwise, uninformed, or even prejudiced, yet other things being equal, the advice of a Christian is to be given special weight. Christians can be guided by the Spirit. If you are having difficulty discerning the inner voice of the Spirit, a godly friend may be the one God uses to assist you.

11. *Don't overlook the counsel of those who know you best.* They may not know the total situation, but they do know you. However, they may not be aware of the special enablement God desires to give you. A long-time prayer partner may be of great help to you.

12. *In evaluating the counsel of others, ask questions.* Weigh the advice of others in the light of questions such as these:

    a. Is the person a Spirit-filled believer?
    b. Is the person mature?
    c. Does the person have special competency in the matter on which you need advice?
    d. Is the person unbiased and open to a variety of views?
    e. Is the person sufficiently acquainted with you and with the situation to be able to advise wisely?

Group Counsel

In group situations God can give guidance through any of its members. Paul was given a vision, and the team ("we") concluded what God's will was (Acts 16:10). The senior person is not necessarily the one through whom God will work. At times a very new Christian or a very young person may be especially sensitive to the voice of the Spirit or be chosen by God for this role.

God can give group consensus through a process in which no one dominates, but several are used, or in which all unitedly without any conscious leader come to the same conviction. I have known most of the members of a committee to receive the same unexpected guidance during a season of prayer when no one mentioned it aloud. Such guidance must be given special weight.

At the Jerusalem Council (Acts 15) there was first "much discussion" (v. 7). Peter then made a statement (vv. 7–11). Paul and Barnabas added their testimonies (v. 12). James summarized their consensus (vv. 13–21). The whole church then united behind the decision (v. 22) and put the decision in writing (vv. 23–29).

All God's children are competent to counsel one another (Rom. 15:14). All are to teach and admonish one another. "Let the word of Christ dwell in you richly as you teach and admonish one another with all wisdom" (Col. 3:16). Notice that this counsel depends on the word of Christ—that is, the teaching and "the mind of Christ" pervading and penetrating all their understanding. *You* may be understood in two ways: Certainly the Word must dwell deeply in the "you" receiving the special guidance; it must also dwell deeply in the whole group to help them arrive at a consensus. Note also that this counsel may be positive (teaching) or negative (admonishing, warning).

When a whole group is seeking God's guidance, follow the same basic principles as for individual guidance. Dr. Paul Rees has advised the following steps:

—Look to Scripture for light.

—Have a period of silence in which each person prayerfully seeks to listen to the voice of the Spirit.

—Have a sharing time when all in turn tell what they believe the Spirit said to them.

—Seek to reach a consensus among the group that all will own as their own decision.

possible hindrances
to guidance, part 1

Have you been perplexed why you have not received God's guidance more often? Remember, you do not need God's guidance in everything. Ask four questions before you seek special guidance.

When You Don't Need Special Guidance

1. Is it in the Bible? Don't ask God to guide you about a matter clearly taught in the Bible. For a Christian to marry an unsaved person is always wrong (2 Cor. 6:14). It is always wrong to do wrong with the motive to bring a good result (Rom. 3:8). It is always wrong to retaliate, to repay evil for evil (Rom. 12:17, 19; 1 Peter 3:9). You need no further guidance in any matter on which the Bible speaks.

2. Is it a duty? Don't waste God's time about a plain duty. It is always duty to pay back what you owe (Rom. 13:8), to show proper respect (1 Peter 2:17)—including the husband to the wife (1 Peter 3:7) and the wife to the husband (Eph. 5:33). It is always your duty to help the poor (Acts 10:4, 31; 2 Cor. 9:9; Gal. 2:10).

3. Is it morally wrong? Moral wrong is never God's will. It is always morally wrong to wish evil (Luke 6:45), to join a group with a rebellious purpose (Prov. 24:21), to approve a moral wrong, to be silent when your witness is needed.

4. Is it common sense? Don't ask God's guidance when sanctified common sense provides an adequate answer. Common sense tells you that helping an injured person takes priority over being on time. Common sense guides you to show love to any child who needs someone's interest, or not to endanger yourself by picking up a hitchhiker unless the Lord specially guides you.

Possible Hindrances

God always has the word you need when you need it. The following questions may help you to discover why you have not been conscious of God's guidance more often.

1. Is some personal sin blocking your prayer and deafening your ear? A controversy between you and the Lord will interfere. When you walk in the light, your fellowship makes hearing God possible (1 John 1:7). Walk in the light God has already given if you want further light from Him.

David wrote, "If I had cherished sin in my heart, the Lord would not have listened" (Ps. 66:18). If you have disobeyed, you first need to repent and ask forgiveness (Deut. 1:45). Isaiah said the Lord's ear was not too dull to hear prayer but "your sins have hidden his face from you so that he will not hear" (Isa. 59:2). Make sure no sin hinders your prayer (1 John 3:22).

2. Do you have the wrong motive? Why do you desire God's guidance? Is it to be a success? Is it to vindicate past actions? Is it to prove you are spiritual? In many subtle ways self and pride can hinder your prayer for guidance. James warned, "When you ask you do not receive, because you ask with wrong motives" (James 4:3).

Personal desire can be a legitimate motive. God has spent time in developing your personality. Holy and appropriate desires are probably from the Spirit. To disregard these would be wrong. Holy desire can be a strong motive and an important factor in the success of what you do according to the will of God. Such desire is an important factor in your decision-making process.

Recognize your desires for what they are. A Spirit-filled person seeks to avoid being influenced by carnal, self-centered desires. Wrong desires bring confusion in discerning the voice of the Spirit. It is proper to consider your personal needs, but balance this by a willingness for self-denial.

Personal need can be a legitimate motive. There will be personal blessing and perhaps benefit if your prayer is answered. But personal benefit must not be the primary motive. Your overriding desire must be for God's will, God's glory, and God's kingdom, regardless of the consequences for you.

3. Has it been difficult for God to get your attention? You may be oblivious to some of the Spirit's attempts to speak to you. This happens most often to those who do not daily hunger to be guided. You may be so absorbed in your concern that you are not keenly aware of God's nearness and voice.

Elijah had been mightily used of God on Mount Carmel. He had been led and sealed by God's miracle signs and miracle power upon him. However, he became so physically and emotionally exhausted that depression came. He ran for his life and prayed God to let him die. God twice awakened Elijah and gave him miraculous bread and water. By God's miracle sustenance Elijah traveled forty days and nights.

God's miracle hand was on him, but Elijah was so obsessed with the nation's need, the wicked rulers, and his problems that he sensed no guidance. Reaching Mount Horeb, he slept in a cave. God spoke to him, but he was so discouraged that he asked no guidance. God displayed His power in tornado, earthquake, and fire to get Elijah's attention and renew his faith. Then in a "gentle whisper" God spoke. Once Elijah was physically refreshed, strengthened in his faith, and alert to the Lord, a whisper was all it took to guide him (1 Kings 19:12).

Your problem may be that you are so absorbed in your real and overwhelming troubles that you have difficulty getting a heart quiet enough and expectant enough to hear God's gentle whisper.

4. Are you truly filled with the Spirit? Every Christian is indwelled by the Holy Spirit. However, many Christians give so little place to the Spirit that He finds it difficult to speak to them and to guide them. When you are truly Spirit-filled you will live "according to the Spirit" (Rom. 8:4), "by the Spirit" (Gal. 5:16).

To be Spirit-filled you must be totally committed to God and His will. Then the sanctifying Spirit can cleanse you of carnal self-centeredness and flood you with His holy presence. Total commitment and absolute surrender give the Spirit complete access to your thoughts, desires, and inner being. He makes you far more sensitive to His voice, will, and desires. If you are struggling with some aspect of the will of God, you often miss the deeper, sweeter ministry of the Spirit. The fullness of the Spirit gives you potential openness to all He would say to you. Perhaps what you need above all else is to be filled with the Spirit.

5. *Are you depending too largely on yourself?* The spirit of this age teaches one to be independent and self-reliant. It is easy to live for days without asking the Lord's guidance in your daily activities.

At the beginning of each day and repeatedly throughout your day, whisper a prayer, committing yourself, asking Him to guide, and thanking Him for His help. Then, unless He gives you an inner hesitation, go along normally.

When you forget to invite the Lord continually into your normal activities, you make little mistakes, waste your time and resources, and lose the listening ear.

6. *Is your mind already made up about what you want to do?* Are you guilty of wanting endorsement for what you have made up your mind to do? You want Him to bless your plans, rather than your discovering His plans. Jeremiah 42–43 records how the leaders came to Jeremiah to ask God's guidance about going to Egypt, when they had already made up their minds. They were trying to "use God" for their own ends. Jeremiah called this a fatal mistake (Jer. 42:20–21). Don't insult God by asking His guidance when your mind is already made up.

7. *Is prejudice hindering you from being neutral?* It is very human to be influenced by prejudice. Satan tries to take advantage of our "natural" biases of religion, blood relationship, past associations and experiences, geographical ties, or linguistic connections.

Prejudice can color your listening to what God says and how you gather and interpret facts. You are more ready to believe some people than others, to discount some reports before you have adequately checked them out. You assume you have sufficient information so that you don't need to double-check the facts.

Even Spirit-filled people can be surprisingly prejudiced. If you think you are immune, you do not truly know yourself. The counsel of mature Spirit-filled people is always helpful.

Many kinds of impressions can prejudice you: first impressions, or impressions of appearance, poverty, cultural differences, group membership, a reputation established before conversion (for example, Saul of Tarsus), past failure (John Mark), or physique (David compared with his brothers). Parental partiality can influence (Jacob and Rachel).

Satan exaggerates, misinforms, and falsely accuses. He is ready to spread rumors. You can be influenced by him without your realizing it.

The Holy Spirit can help free you from prejudice, but it will require alertness and self-discipline. Take extra time to pray when you know prejudice might be influencing you. Seek godly counsel from someone who knows you and the situation well and is willing to be honest with you. God can guide you in spite of a tendency toward prejudice or jumping to conclusions.

8. *Are your desires so strong that discerning God's guidance is difficult?* In the full commitment required for the Holy Spirit to fill you, all controversy between the Lord and you is settled. But there may be areas where His will is not yet clear and your desires are so strong that you may not be completely neutral.

Even after you are Spirit-cleansed you will have strong requests, desires, and preferences. You are free to express these desires to the Lord, but then surrender them to Him. Your heart is rarely quiet enough to hear God's voice until these recognized preferences are fully surrendered to whatever God may desire.

possible hindrances to guidance, part 2

In light of God's promise to give you a word whenever you need it, we must explore additional reasons why you have not at times been conscious of receiving His guidance.

9. Are you trying to bargain with God? Jacob tried this. He prayed that if God would go with him, protect him, give him food and clothing, and bring him back safely, then he would serve Him. God in His mercy took care of Jacob, but there is no record of Jacob's being greatly guided by the Lord.

You must be totally committed to the Lord and serve Him totally, exuberantly, and faithfully whether or not He leads you in paths you would yourself choose. When you serve thus, regardless of your preference, you can trust for His continuous guidance.

10. Do you tend to act prematurely? Don't rush into decisions and actions before you should. Be patient enough to wait when action is not immediately called for. Is waiting on God difficult for you? Do you gather sufficient evidence? Does waiting make you fretful? Do you act before God's perfect time arrives?

Trust God to guide not only in what to do but when to do it. There is not only the better way, but also the better time—God's time. Wait for Him to guide you.

11. Do you desire too strongly some highly unusual or spectacular form of guidance? God has at times used these for special reasons. They were more necessary before the Bible was written and the

Holy Spirit sent to indwell us. They were more necessary to prove that Jehovah was the living God in contrast to the gods of the pagans, or that Christ was the Son of God. God uses such means more frequently today on mission fields, where the same need of proof is important for non-Christians.

God often stoops to your level to strengthen your faith, give assurance, or confirm His will. But we live in the dispensation of the Spirit. He is to be your primary Guide and Counselor. You are to listen for His voice. You have no right to demand special dramatic forms of guidance regularly.

The more mature you become in Christ, the more naturally God guides you by the inner assurance and inner voice of the Spirit. The more closely you follow Christ, the more you as His sheep recognize His voice (John 10:3, 5, 27). Only rarely do you need more dramatic means. Your life is a life of faith. By having simple trust and a listening ear as your "lifestyle," you learn to make guidance normal, natural, and your daily privilege.

The Devil can counterfeit dreams, visions, miracles, prophecies, and similar manifestations that we normally expect only God to use. The supernatural is not necessarily a proof of God. The occult and the cults are often marked by such counterfeits. Scripture instructs us to test the spirits (1 John 4:1). Check to see if the guidance is in full harmony with scriptural truth, is associated with holy lives, is reasonable and right, and is accompanied by deep, inner peace and assurance.

12. Do you depend too much on the counsel of others? Do you fail to seek God's will first and go to special advisers prematurely? It is always dangerous to put God in second place. No matter how expert your counselor, if you feel a strong inner urge to one action or a restraint in your inner spirit about that action, place the priority on the Lord's counsel.

Paul consulted with Peter and James (Gal. 1:18–19) and with the leaders of the Jerusalem church fourteen years later (Gal. 2:1–2). "I did this privately to those who seemed to be leaders, for fear that I was running or had run my race in vain" (v. 2).

There are occasions, however, when you are so sure of guidance that you obey God's leading even when other Christians do not understand. Paul had to deal with Peter this way (Gal. 2:11–21). Welcome counsel, but depend primarily on God.

13. *Do you have difficulty recognizing God's voice?* Probably the most prevalent form of divine guidance is an inner impression. Perhaps the most common form of restraint is an inner hesitation. But how do you distinguish between impressions from the Holy Spirit and other impressions? Check again the guidelines offered in chapter 25.

14. *Are you influenced by your emotions?* You are always in danger of mistaking your own emotions for the inner assurance of the Spirit. This is because your feelings, biases, preferences, and desires are so much a part of your personality. Emotions may mislead you in many matters, but particularly when you are seeking God's will regarding marriage. Here the wise counsel of a discerning spiritual friend can be very helpful.

Personal attraction can have such profound emotional overtones that you might fail to hear the Spirit's voice or even the voice of your reason and common sense. Health, excessive weariness, deep disappointments, certain medications—these can profoundly influence you negatively. Emotions are notoriously changeable.

On the one hand, the emotions of deep spiritual joy and deep inner peace are a part of God's seal on your obedience, a part of His witness to your soul. The more you follow the guidance of the Spirit, the deeper the joy and peace become, even when outward circumstances are still confusing and difficult.

On the other hand, if there is no physical or other obvious reason, a continuing inner lack of peace and joy may be an indication that the Spirit is trying to restrain you. Wait further before the Lord in prayer. God does not expect you to act while you are in a state of confusion. He speaks clearly.

when God is silent

Throughout Scripture God is pictured as the speaking God, the God who hears and answers prayer. Nothing is more common to Christian experience than this assurance. This is our joyous testimony to unsaved people and a non-Christian world. Our God is alive; our God answers prayer.

Nothing is more heart searching to a Christian than a period when it suddenly seems that this joyous Christian testimony is thrown into question because God seems temporarily to be silent. If you have faced such perplexing times in your life, you are not alone.

During Job's intense trial, while he was crying to God day and night, his most heart-searching pain was probably not the calamities that struck him blow after blow, but the silence of God to his prayer and complaint.

> Though I cry . . . I get no response (Job 19:7).

> If only I knew where to find him; if only I could go to his dwelling!. . . . But if I go to the east, he is not there; if I go to the west, I do not find him. When he is at work in the north, I do not see him; when he turns to the south, I catch no glimpse of him (23:3, 8–9).

David also wrestled with the silence of God. "My God, my God, why have you forsaken me? Why are you so far from saving me, so far from the words of my groaning? O my God, I cry out by day, but you do not answer, by night, and am not silent" (Ps. 22:1–2). This is the psalm Jesus quoted on the cross (Matt. 27:46). In fact, a number of the verses of this psalm are an exact description of the sufferings of Christ at Calvary. David's experience of God's silence and God's seeming distance prepared him to voice prophetically the very words of the Son of God.

Elsewhere David pleads with God not to be deaf and silent to his cry (Ps. 28:1), not to be silent and far away (35:22). "O God, do not keep silent; be not quiet, O God, be not still" (83:1). Others saw the psalmist's unanswered need while he was crying to God day and night and taunted him, "Where is your God?" (42:3). Indeed, the psalmist asked God, "Why have you forgotten me?" (42:9). Three times he asks in identical words, "Why are you downcast, O my soul? Why so disturbed within me?" (42:5, 11; 43:5).

Periods of God's silence, when God seemed far away, were known to saints in both Old and New Testament times, and to Christ on the cross. Each person's situation is different, but for each one the pain of the silence is real, soul searching, and unexplained. No one can ever write a book which will answer your deepest questions about God's silences in your life; the silences are too personal.

In the preceding two chapters we have considered possible hindrances to guidance. They are your checklist to make sure the silence is unrelated to any step you need to take. Now let me share suggestions to remember while you await God's voice again.

While You Wait in the Silence

1. God is as near to you as He ever was. There is nothing God would rather do than lavish His love upon you and thrill you with joy and blessing. He longs to overwhelm you with manifestations and assurances of His loving presence. He is as near you as He has ever been. He only seems to be deaf; He hears every sigh, every longing, every cry of your heart. He longs to speak, but His temporary silence is necessary to the great result and reward He is planning for you. He seems to be far away; you seem to be forgotten and forsaken. But His loving eye is upon you constantly, and His loving arms, though unseen, are holding you and surrounding you all the time (Deut. 33:27).

2. God's silence is always temporary. While you are passing through the silence, the time seems long. Be assured that God has already set a terminal point and that the end of His silence is approaching. It is God's nature to speak; He will speak again to you. God is covenanted to you, and His covenant of love is unchangeable.

3. Your questions will be answered by God. His answer will completely satisfy you. He has chosen for you what you would choose for yourself if you could see the whole as God sees it. Job is completely satisfied with God's answer today, though he did not get a complete answer while he lived. David could not understand why he had to hide and run for his life for seven years and risk death over and over when God had already anointed him to be king. You and I still don't know David's complete answer, but David does and is completely satisfied.

Earth has no questions that heaven will not answer. You may not have to wait until eternity to get your full answer. God gives us many answers comparatively soon after we ask them, but if not before, you are sure of a total answer in heaven. God is a fellowshiping, speaking, answering, and rewarding God.

4. Make no changes while God is silent. Someone has said, "Never try to change trains while passing through a tunnel." Never make a decision while you are discouraged, sensing great darkness, or feeling depressed. You will probably live to regret any decision that you make at such a time. You were walking in the path of God's guidance. The silence has changed nothing. Your unanswered question has changed nothing. The dark silence has not changed you, God, or the situation.

Since God has led you to the place where you are, it would be unwise to make any change until God gives you new directions as clearly as He gave you the original guidance. God is duty bound by His character to alert you in time to make any change He plans for you (Isa. 30:20–21).

Let me repeat, a father is far more responsible to give an obedient child new directions at the proper time than the child is responsible to know that a new direction is needed. Your indwelling Counselor is more responsible to direct you than you are to ask

Him for directions. When God is silent He expects you to continue as you are until He speaks again.

5. *Reexamine your priorities.* While God is silent, you should spend prayerful time reexamining the priorities of your life and of the decision before you. Perhaps God is purposely giving you time to think. Examine your priorities in the light of these realities:

    a. God's past guidance
    b. Eternal values
    c. Your goals
    d. Your remaining span of life
    e. Your family and loved ones
    f. Your church and friends
    g. Any other checkpoints that God brings to your attention

You live but once. Are you living wisely? Are you doing those things that in eternity will bring you the greatest satisfaction?

6. *Check your obedience.* Have you been forgetting some of the past guidance God gave you? Have you been walking in His light? This is the key to the fellowship with God you need for continual guidance (1 John 1:7). Are there any specific steps of obedience you could take to prepare the way for God's answer to your prayer?

In particular, is there anyone who holds something against you? Broken relationships can be a major cause of God's silence. In all strained relationships there is usually some fault on both sides. But even if you are faultless, you are the one responsible to take the initiative, according to Matthew 5:23–24. When you have humbly and graciously taken that step, you are free in God's sight, and heaven may soon open to you again.

7. *Saturate your soul with Scripture.* This is a major priority for you when God is silent. There is no more certain way to hear the voice of God than by listening to what He has already spoken in His Word. Plan your time so that in some quiet place you can read on and on in Scripture. Try spending an hour or even two each day reading God's Word—not devotional books, as good as they may be. There is no substitute for the Bible itself. You are more apt to hear God's guidance when you read God's Word than in anything else you do. Try it. Saturate your soul in the Word.

8. *Plan a personal prayer retreat.* Perhaps you have not been

spending enough time alone with God. Saturating your soul with the Word should be accompanied by extra time for prayer. You may want to set your alarm and arise earlier each day to spend time in prayer. Perhaps you can isolate yourself from the phone and social contacts for a longer time in the evening.

Probably the most helpful way to find God's will after a time of His silence is to plan a personal prayer retreat alone with Him for at least a day. Everyone needs personal prayer retreats like this once or twice a year, as God guides and as you can arrange the time and place. When God is silent, a personal prayer retreat can be much used of the Lord to help you (see appendix A).

Plan such a retreat. You will feel closer to God and full of new praise, faith, and expectancy. You will probably be so blessed that you will want to plan more retreat times.

What If God Is Still Silent?

God's silence will usually end during your prayer retreat. But you may find that some of the issues or the main issue you had before Him is still not clear. Is God still being silent on that particular matter?

Keep living in God's Word, praising Him for His goodness and faithfulness, and expressing your personal love to Him. Rest quietly in His faithfulness. The responsibility to act is His. His way is best. Give God time to work further in your life and in the lives of others. Keep on obeying and serving Him as you are doing now.

You may have a blind spot. Perhaps God's silence is your answer in the matter you have been praying about. This is more likely true if He is speaking to you, answering you, and using you in other matters but keeping silent in regard to this particular concern. Commit your way to the Lord, and go forward in other aspects of His will and guidance.

aRE you called?

What does it mean to be "called by God"? Can a person be called as a secretary, a scientist, a medical doctor, or a nurse? Have you been confused by the conflicting advice of well-meaning Bible teachers, missionary speakers, or Christian workers?

You Are Called

God's plan for your life, or any part of that plan, is sometimes called "God's call," or "God's will." Many people are almost afraid to use the word *call* in reference to themselves. If you study the Bible's use of this word, you will find that the call of God means the same thing as the will of God. Search a concordance and see for yourself. Everything that is God's will for you is His call for you. Just as you can know the will of God, so you can know His call.

1. *Every Christian is called by God.* Every Christian has many calls by God. There is God's comprehensive salvation call, His call to holy living, His call to future sharing in Christ's glory and heaven's rewards, and His call that relates to your vocation and situation in life. The term *call* can be applied to any part of God's will for you. God says we are "those whom God has called" (1 Cor. 1:24), "those who are called" (Heb. 9:15), and those "who have been called according to His purpose" (Rom. 8:28).

God's salvation call is to repentance (Luke 5:32), out of darkness into God's wonderful light (1 Peter 2:9), by the grace of

Christ (Gal. 1:6), to peace (Col. 3:15), to freedom (Gal. 5:13), to fellowship with Christ (1 Cor. 1:9), and to eternal life (1 Tim. 6:12). Having been called to belong to Jesus Christ (Rom. 1:6), you are then called to live in holiness (1 Thess. 4:7; 2 Tim. 1:9), to be a saint (Rom. 1:7), to be godly (2 Peter 1:3), and to inherit blessing (1 Peter 3:9).

God calls you to one great hope (Eph. 4:4), which includes all His plans for your future. You are called to His eternal kingdom and glory (1 Thess. 2:12; 1 Peter 5:10), to share in the glory of our Lord Jesus Christ (2 Thess. 2:14), and to share God's heavenly rewards (Phil. 3:14).

You should therefore live worthy of His calling (2 Thess. 1:11; Eph. 4:1). God's whole scheme of grace is described as your heavenly calling (Heb. 3:1), although by obedience you must eagerly make your calling sure (2 Peter 1:10).

2. Every Christian is called to service. God's general call to service is for everyone, and each of us has a specially assigned place of service. Each is a particular part of Christ's body and has a special function (1 Cor. 12:27). Each is a part of God's building (1 Cor. 3:9) and has his own place (1 Peter 2:5). Each is to be Christ's salt in a decaying civilization (Matt. 5:13), His light in a world of spiritual darkness (Matt. 5:14). Each is a branch of the vine and is to yield fruit to God (John 15:5). Each is a part of God's field and is therefore to yield a harvest for God (1 Cor. 3:9).

Every Christian is as much sent by Christ as Christ was sent by the Father (John 20:21). Everyone who has responded to His call to "come" is responsible to His command to "go." The "Lo, I am with you" is for those who obey the call to "go" in the preceding verse (Matt. 28:19–20). We are not all called to go to the same persons or places, but we are all called to go. No one is excused.

Everyone who receives the fullness of the Spirit (Acts 1:8) is to be a witness from his Jerusalem to the ends of the earth. We are to begin by going to our home community (our Jerusalem), but we are not to stop until we reach the ends of the earth. But we are not all called to go in the same way. All are called to go to the whole world in their prayer and as far as possible in their giving. Some are called to go in person.

Any Christian who does not have world vision and world

prayer burden is falling short of the glory of God. But no one should either go or stay unless he feels he is doing it in the will of God. You are already called to be Christ's witness where you are; it may be that He will call you to be His witness in some distant part of His harvest field. But if you are failing to witness where you are now, you are failing God as much as if you failed to go to a foreign field when you knew that was His will. You are called to His service where you are. The only questions are how far God plans to send you in His service and whether that service is part-time or full-time.

3. *No one can take your place*. No one can ever fully do your work for you. God has given you a background, a special set of personal experiences of His faithfulness, and a personality, and He has invested His mercy and grace in you in such a way that you can bless some people better than anyone else ever could. You are God's most perfect instrument for some tasks. You have your own role to play in the plan of God, and no one else can take your place.

You are needed by God for the task for which He is preparing you. It will take all your love, prayer, and faithfulness to fulfill God's call and will for you. If I leave part of my work undone and you fill my place, then you leave empty the place God wanted you to fill and some of the work God wanted you to do will be left undone. None of us has a right to conclude, "Well, if I don't obey God, someone else will take my place." If you fail to obey God, there will be a gap in the work of God (Ezek. 22:30). There are many unfilled gaps in the work of God around the world today.

4. *Keep your hands pure of men's blood*. Your accountability for another is referred to in the Bible as "blood." When you fail to obey God and fulfill His plan for your life, or if you refuse His will and call, God holds you responsible for the blood of those you would have reached had you obeyed Him. If you fail to be God's watchman where He needs you, you may be saved yourself, but your hands will be stained with the blood of others (read Ezek. 33:6–9).

Paul's great concern was that he keep his hands innocent of the blood of all men (Acts 18:6; 20:26–27). If you fail to put first things first and waste life in trivial things, if you fail God's purpose and have only second best, you may build your life on the foundation, Jesus Christ (1 Cor. 3:10–11), but build with wood, hay, and straw instead of with gold, silver, and precious stones (v. 12). The judgment day will prove that though your soul was saved, your life's work was largely burned up (vv. 13–14). Your life will have been at least partially wasted and you will suffer loss (v. 15). God forbid that your soul be saved but your life lost!

You Can Know God's Will Clearly

God calls you because He wants you to know His will. He is far more anxious to show you His will than you are to know it. He is your Father! He loves you. He is planning what is best for you. No human father has ever been so anxious to explain to his child as God is anxious to make His will clear to you. He longs to be gracious to you. He longs to use you. He longs for you to understand clearly and exactly what He is calling you to do.

As long as you desire to know His will you are sure to find it. The only one who misses God's will and call is the one who is careless and disobedient. If you do not constantly seek to know His will and walk step by step in the light He gives you, naturally you will miss part of God's plan. But if you truly long to know and do His will, He will make it plain. God, your loving Father, wants you to relax in His love, in the assurance that He takes the responsibility for your life and will make His call clear to you.

As long as you don't know, wait! Do not worry; do not get under pressure and fear. If you are rejoicing in His love, gladly obeying Him the best you know how, but do not yet know God's call, just wait. God has been guiding you thus far. You are today in the place where you are because of God's providence and grace. Hold steady, and in God's best time He will make the next step plain to you.

In the meantime He is preparing the place for you and you for the place. God is just as responsible to make His will plain to you as you are to obey it. He knows you do not fully understand His will yet. He has deliberately brought you to this place. Now keep trusting and obeying and watch how He guides you step by step. You will always know His will in plenty of time.

Wrong Concepts of God's Call

It can be confusing to listen to what some say about God's call. Well-meaning, spiritual people can give confusing and wrong advice. Here are some mistaken theories about the call of God.

1. *"You don't need a call."* Some well-meaning people have said, "What are you waiting for? You don't need a call." How completely unscriptural! You as a Christian are already called by God in many ways. God plans for you to serve Him. It is not a question of needing a call. Rather, where does God need you? Where and how can you best serve Him?

2. *"The need is the call."* Again, how completely unbiblical! God's will is God's call. God calls you to meet need, but the need is not the call. There are a multitude of urgent, unmet needs. A similar wrong question is, where is the greatest need? The real question is, where does God need you most? He wants to get you to that place where He needs you!

3. *"The open door is the call."* This is a half-truth. God will always open the door so you can fulfill His call. But the open door is not the call. For the person who keeps close to God, obeys God, and blesses others, there arc probably more doors open than he has time or strength to enter. Day by day you need God's guidance in what is most important for that day.

Furthermore, Satan often seeks to close the door to the work to which God calls you. The door may be closed until God's time comes, but then His miracle power opens the way. You never have to knock down a door to obey God. If you do, you are out of God's will. Jesus keeps the key. It is His responsibility to open the door before you when you do His will. If He keeps the door locked, He does not want you to enter that door yet.

God's Call Is an Inner Assurance

God's call is His inner assurance in your heart. People have received this assurance in many ways. Just as one testimony to the new birth is different from every other, so every testimony to the call is different. A few people have received a vision, but that is very rare. The vision was not the call; the vision was a special additional witness God granted to seal the call. Sometimes God uses a message or a book to get the heart into an attitude where He can make His call clear; but that message or book is not the call. God has at times used the counsel of a godly pastor or friend to help make His will clear; but no human being can give you God's call.

God's call is always the inner assurance He gives within your heart that some definite step is His will for you. He may seal this call through providence, through godly friends, or by some other means. But it is the inner assurance that counts—it is another form of the witness of the Spirit. The Spirit witnesses to your salvation; He also witnesses to God's will for your life.

A Call to Christian Service?

1. God's call usually proceeds from the general to the specific. No one knows at one time all God's purpose for his life. There are always steps in knowing God's will and plan. There may be first a clear sense that God's hand is on your life, that He wants you to serve Him in some special way or in some form of full-time service.

It may be an inner assurance that God is calling to overseas missionary service. Sometimes God immediately makes the country clear, but often He gives that guidance in a later step. Let God follow His own sequence and plan in making His call clear, but if He is calling you to be a missionary you can be sure that sooner or later He will guide you and make His will, His call, His plan clear for you in all these steps: (a) the country, (b) the type of work, (c) the society or mission, (d) the preparation to be made, and (e) the life's companion—if He calls you to go as a married person. (Sometimes God calls two people to go as single persons and then calls the two together into marriage after they are on the field.)

2. God's call is always progressive. God leads step by step. God may call you to new types of service. He may call you to further training. He may call you to new steps of faith and obedience that you have never thought of before. You do not know today all that God's call will involve a month or a year from today. God will be faithful and make each step clear before you.

His call involves daily guidance and obedience. Every day has new opportunities and new responsibilities; every day you need the guidance, anointing, and enabling of His Spirit. What a joy, what a holy thrill and romance there is in living for God and letting God use your life in any way He will, opening doors before you as He puts His seal upon your life!

Yes, God is calling you to serve Him. It may be in a full-time capacity; it may be to continue in your regular vocation. It is always to make every opportunity count for God and the extension of His kingdom. Be open to any aspect of His will, any call. It is probably equally as important to know God's call *not* to go into full-time Christian service as it is to know God's call *into* such service. You cannot take either for granted.

Steps You Can Take to Discover God's Call

1. Be sure you are totally surrendered to God's will. Reaffirm to God your total surrender to His will whatever it may be and whenever He may choose. Make sure yours is an eternal "yes" in advance to God for all your tomorrows, a decisive and final commitment of your will to Him. Hereafter it will not be a question of "if," but only of "what, when, and how?" From now on you are open, available and only waiting for His assignment.

2. Live in the fullness of the Spirit. Be sure you have been filled with the Spirit; then keep open to His continual refilling, controlling, equipping, guiding, anointing, and using you. Keep hungry for and expect more of His presence, for Him to guide, empower, and use you. By faith appropriate more of His Spirit each day.

3. Be active for the Lord. Seek to be useful now in every way possible. Bless as many as possible each day. Show your Christian love, eagerness to help, and constant dependence on the Lord. Make use of daily prayer lists—the unsaved, your church, your nation, Christian and missionary organizations, nations needing Christ. Contribute to God's cause at home and abroad. Be active in witnessing and serving. Begin leading people to Christ now.

4. Begin any preparation you may need. If your desires, skills, or experience suggest any particular vocation, see what further training you can pursue now. Whatever your vocation, you need to know God's Word. Take advantage of Bible classes, Bible study courses, or Bible teaching books. Keep reading God's Word extensively. In full-time Christian service you will probably need special Bible training in addition to whatever college or technical training you have. The organization with which you serve will guide you concerning any special training needed.

5. Take actions to discover God's will. If you are considering Christian service, consider the overwhelming disproportion in the number of people serving Christ in the English-speaking world compared with the small number in some of the most unreached mission fields. Take the initiative in gathering information and praying about opportunities and needs.

Learn about Christian organizations that have the kind of ministry toward which you feel led or in which you have interest. Check out their doctrine, their reputation in Christian circles, the stability of the organization, the level of supervision and support of their members, the extent to which the home base provides prayer support and keeps prayer-partners adequately informed. Do they cooperate with other Christian groups, or are they separatistic? Make use of opportunities to hear missionary speakers or attend conventions and special events of evangelical organizations.

6. *Keep listening for the Spirit's voice.* Keep thanking God for all He is planning for your life. Keep renewing your commitment, reminding Him of your availability. Keep filling your soul with God's Word and investing time daily in intercession. Set apart a brief time each day when you pray about God's will. Schedule a personal prayer retreat as outlined in appendix A. Keep trusting, praising, and obeying the Lord. Keep watching for any doors He may open before you, or doors where He leads you to knock. Relax in your Father's love, your Counselor's faithfulness, and the certainty that God will guide you step by step as long as you are active for Him and diligently seeking to know His will.

aRe you called to missions? of couRse!

You a missionary? Why not? You personally sharing in world harvest? Of course! Every Christian—I repeat, everyone—is called to share in one or more ways in Christ's great and final command. He wants to reach everyone alive today with the gospel.

Certainly this involves planned, daily prayer participation. God wants more from you than a brief "God bless the missionaries" sometime during your daily prayer. God wants you to be involved in definite intercession daily. You need God's guidance on how to plan your specific prayer involvement in God's program and strategy to reach His world now.

Additionally, God is calling every Christian to some personal financial commitment supporting world harvest. World evangelism is God's top priority and must become ours. If you are a member of a church with a lively, active program of missions, you may be able to fulfill God's guidance in giving through it. Or God may guide you to special, additional regular investment in this cause.

We will always face tremendously touching cases of tragedy, poverty, and need in some part of the world. Chronic situations in some nations will always cry for help. A Christlike person wants to share. But the priority is always that people receive Christ and spend eternity with Him in heaven. Supporting relief projects is important, but can never displace God's priority of evangelism. Be sure that world evangelism is in your giving.

None of that involvement, however, may excuse you from personal action in some other way. Does God have a full-time assignment for you in a cross-cultural outreach and harvest? Whether you are a youth or a retiree, whatever your role in life, God may have a special place where He desires to use you for a shorter or longer time. There are many options available today.

People committed to lifelong involvement are always the foundation and backbone of missions outreach. God give us more! But there are places where you may be needed for a week, ten days, a month, a summer, or even a year or two. Would you let God guide you to give up your vacation or a longer period to go where you can use your skill and experience, or give just the little additional help that's needed?

God has greatly used witnessing groups or assistance groups who have gone to another nation for a short time to help repair mission buildings, assist in painting or construction, or to help with camping programs. Hundreds of students each year spend some weeks teaching English as a second language and sharing their Christian witness. What can you do? Is God waiting for you?

Does God Want You to Go?

As a Christian you have no right to assume that God does not want you to share in missionary service with those of another culture or language until you have asked Him and found His clear guidance one way or the other. But before you begin seriously to pray about it, consider some striking facts. Did you know that

—World population increases by more than 200,000 a day? (*U.S. News & World Report*, 23 July 1984)
—There were about 250 million people on earth when Jesus was born? It took from Adam to 1850 for earth's population to reach one billion. In only eighty years it reached two billion (1930). In thirty more years it reached three (1960), and seventeen after that (1977), four billion (*U.S. News & World Report*, 28 March 1977). Ten years later, the world population reached five billion (1987). By the year 2000 it will be about 6.3 billion. In the past ten years the earth's population has increased as much as it did from Adam to 1850. That is a population explosion!

—Probably one-fourth of the world has never heard the name of Jesus so as to understand what it means, and another one-fourth has heard it but not enough to know how to be saved? Thus one-half of the world has had no genuine opportunity to receive Christ (Bishop Stephen Neill).

—Eighty-three percent of the world has no indigenous church? (Ralph Winter)

—Seven out of eight Christians have never had a complete Bible in their own language? (Don Hillis)

—If all the unsaved people would line up single file in front of your door, the line would reach around the earth thirty times? It would continue to grow twenty miles a day! If you drove your car from your door nonstop at fifty miles an hour, ten hours a day, it would take you four years and forty days to reach the point where the line originally ended, but by that time it would be 30,000 miles longer (Free Methodist bulletin to pastors).

—America, with 5 percent of the world's population, has more ordained ministers, more Christian radio stations, and more Bible college students than the rest of the world altogether? (*The Church Around the World,* 1977)

—In North America there is one Christian worker per every 1,321 people, in Africa one for every 249,278 persons, but in Asia one for every 2,760,636 people? (*World Christian Encyclopedia,* 1985)

Obviously many people have not been hearing or obeying God's call. Where are the greatest gaps in God's work today? God said through Ezekiel, "I looked for a man among them who would build up the wall and stand before me in the gap on behalf of the land so I would not have to destroy it, but I found none" (Ezek. 22:30). God was longing to be gracious to the land, but He found no one to warn the people of their sin and call them to accept His love and forgiveness.

God is urgently looking for Christians to fill the gaps in His service so that He can be gracious to millions of people who have no chance to know of and accept His love today. The people around you and me have had multiplied opportunities to respond to the gospel, out of all proportion to the rest of the world.

Only God knows where you are needed most, where your life

can count most for Him. But you have no right to assume that God wants you to stay in your own homeland among your own people until you have asked Him the meaning of the overwhelmingly greater need for someone like you to fill His gaps.

Humanly speaking, you could assume that God expected you to go to fill these gaps unless He stopped you. But you need not assume anything. Your life is so precious to God that He has a perfect plan for you. Don't assume anything, but seek His guidance.

On July 16, 1962, while I was being driven across Auckland, New Zealand, and praying about my speaking engagement at the Bible Training Institute, I wrote the following words.

There's a Gap Awaiting You

There's a gap awaiting you;
There is work for you to do.
There's a place which no one else but you can fill.
You are God's own chosen one
For a work that must be done;
God has chosen you according to His will.

There's unfinished work today;
There's a part which you must play.
There's a vacancy awaiting in God's plan.
No one else your work can do;
God's depending now on you.
You and you alone are God's appointed man.

Pause to hear God's voice today;
Listen closely while you pray.
God has something which His Spirit now would speak.
You can find God's perfect will;
All His plan He will fulfill.
You will find it if His will alone you seek.

Follow God whate'er the price,
Though it cost you sacrifice;
It is sweet to know and do the will of God.
There's a gap for you to fill;
Do not miss God's call and will
Lest you stain your conscience and your hands with blood.

During my message I read the poem to the students.

Several months after returning to my ministry at the Allahabad Bible Seminary in Allahabad, India, where I was principal, I received a letter from one of the New Zealand students. She said God had called her to India while I was reading the poem. She asked for a copy, which I sent gladly. Over the next year she wrote to ask various questions, then wrote that she had been accepted for missionary service by a New Zealand board and would soon see me in India.

One day in Allahabad I received another letter in her handwriting. It said, "I am very sorry to inform you that you will never see me in India. I have made a great mistake. Now no board would send me to the mission field." I dropped my head to my hands in grief and began to pray. Then I turned to my bookshelf, chose one of my notebooks of poems, and read again the words she had said God used to call her. I was gripped again by the last three lines:

There's a gap for you to fill;
Do not miss God's call and will
Lest you stain your conscience and your hands with blood.

Oh, the tragedy of people who have missed God's will for their lives!

What Steps Should You Take If God Is Calling You?

1. Thank Him for His loving plan for your life. Thank Him that He is going to make it clear to you step by step.

2. Be completely neutral in your own will and let God guide you any way He desires.

3. Expect Him to make the steps clear one at a time. If it is service in another part of the world, God may be putting a particular nation or a specific type of ministry on your heart. He may begin by leading you to offer yourself to a particular missionary organization and let them decide where they need you most urgently.

4. Expect God to put His seal on your guidance by leading your local church, pastor, or Christian friends to confirm the guidance. Expect God to work out the necessary details step by step by His providence. He rarely makes everything clear at one time, because He is teaching you important lessons of faith over time.

5. Take the steps desirable, as God guides you, to fulfill His call. Learn all you can about the nation or people where He is sending you—about their religion and customs. You will probably need to learn the language after you get there. You may be led to get further, special training important to your ministry. When your appointment is confirmed, which may be a process requiring considerable time, get as many people as possible to commit themselves to daily prayer for you.

When I was just a child, God assured me that He wanted me in India. I always thought I would be an evangelist in some hidden place. Later, during my college days, He led me toward being a teacher in a Bible college. More than a year after that, He confirmed to me the organization under which He wanted me to serve: OMS International.

The final step in God's guidance regarding my ministry came during my first term of service in India. I had gone alone on a mountain to spend a day communing, fasting, and interceding for our work. Suddenly God put it in my heart to complete my doctorate during our furlough. I had never even thought of further training and had no special desire for it. But God made it so clear that I knew it was His will. He worked out all the details and supplied all the funds even though I did not know where they would come from. When God calls us, in His time He will open every needed door before us.

God may guide you to serve under your own denominational board of missions. Or He may guide you to one of the splendid evangelical missionary boards. This is especially possible if your denomination does not have openings for new missionaries or for persons with your qualifications. It is important to God and to you that you make the right decision. Be sure to consider these points:

1. Is the board's standard of doctrine evangelical and agreeable with yours?

2. Does the board have a record of stability, growth, and effective ministry?

3. Does it have the kind of ministry for which you are qualified and to which you feel called?

4. Does it have a record of adequate support for its missionaries? adequate medical assistance in case of need? the funds when you need to come home? Does it provide adequate orientation before you leave for your field of service? Examine its manual carefully to study all its regulations and provisions.

5. *Is it a member of an evangelical missionary accrediting organization?* In the Untied States this would be either the Evangelical Foreign Missions Association (EFMA) or the Interdenominational Foreign Mission Association (IFMA). Membership in these indicates that a board has met certain high standards and is stable, cooperative, and commended by God's people.

The Holy Spirit who calls you will guide you step by step in fulfilling your call. He wants you to be effective, blessed in your service, adequately led by your supporting organization, and fruitful for His glory. When the difficult times come, as they do in all Christian service, then you can look back and thank God that you received clear assurance of His will. You will know that until He changes His assignment to you, you can depend on His blessing ultimately to meet every need.

what if you miss god's will?

It is possible to be outside God's will or to miss His will and guidance in three senses.

1. Personal rebellion. It is possible purposely to disobey God and reject His will for your life. This results in living in sinful conflict with God the Holy Spirit's rebuke to your conscience. Adam and Eve rejected God's will for them in the Garden of Eden. Millions bear a guilty conscience before God today. They know they are not spiritually what God wants them to be. They are deliberately sinning against God's light.

There is only one remedy when you are outside God's will in this rebellious sense. You must turn from your rejection of God's will and in humble repentance ask His forgiveness. God promises forgiveness to anyone who will confess and forsake his sin, trusting in Christ's mercy and grace.

Having been forgiven, you can start life anew in the will of God. God will take you, beginning where you are, and work out a plan for you in His will. But you will have months or years forever lost, for you will lose the reward you might have had if you had only lived in the will of God during that time of sinful rebellion.

2. Major mistakes. It is possible to be aware that you have missed God's will for your life in some of the major decisions you have made. This may include decisions involving marriage, a call to Christian service, education, or vocation. Jonah foolishly tried to run away from God's will. Your missing God's will in a major way may be the result of spiritual neglect on your part, lack of prayerfulness, failure to accept the mature, spiritual counsel of others, failure to enter a door God opened before you, failure to heed the restraint of the Spirit, or some similar reason. It may also be the result of a deliberate, temporary disobedience of God for which you are now repentant. Ask God to take you where you are and work out His best plan from this day on.

3. *Mistakes along the way.* You may have been in the will of God in general, but have taken unwise or unguided steps in some of the specific and perhaps minor details of your life. These may result in more or less unfortunate consequences. Note some examples:

You may have accepted God's call to Christian service but failed to secure adequate training at the proper time. You may have moved to another city in the will of God but unwisely purchased a house in the wrong location. You may have taken a vacation trip without God's guidance and ended up in an accident. You may have maintained a consistent prayer life but failed to set apart a half-day for fasting and prayer as you felt led. As a result you may have missed a special opportunity to counsel a friend or win someone to Christ. Ask God to forgive, and follow more prayerfully.

You Need Not Fear Missing God's Will

Every Christian should have a wholesome concern to please God in everything and not to miss His will and plan. There is always the possibility of missing what is most for God's glory and your good and then experiencing second best. It is because of this possibility that the Holy Spirit is given to be your abiding Counselor (John 14:16) and constant Guide.

To the committed Christian filled with the Spirit and seeking constantly to listen for God's guidance, missing His will in any major decision is not a great danger. You belong to God. He loves you too much and is too committed to you through Calvary to withhold from you the guidance that you need. For you to miss God's will in this sense would be an even greater disappointment to God than to you. God takes the responsibility to see that adequate guidance is available to you.

God does not want you to live in a morbid fear of missing His plan for you. He does not want you to be unwholesomely introspective, repeatedly asking when or why you may have missed His will or failed to be guided aright. God desires you to be a happy Christian, a successful Christian, a person relaxed in your Christian life, walking in close companionship with Him.

It is Satan who puts you under pressure, makes you tense, and seeks to get you in bondage to stress and strain. He wants to enslave you by fear and worry. This is his most effective way to keep you from receiving God's guidance. Satan's bondage is the exact opposite to the spirit of sonship that God wants you to enjoy. "Those who are led by the Spirit of God are sons of God. For you did not receive a spirit that makes you a slave again to fear, but you received the Spirit of sonship" (Rom. 8:14–15).

When Is It Unlikely That You Will Miss God's Will?

It is unlikely that you will miss God's will in a serious or major way when the following conditions exist:

1. *When your will is wholly surrendered to God.*

2. *When you are filled and controlled by the Spirit.*

3. *When you walk in God's light as fully as you understand it.*

4. *When you are reading God's Word extensively and endeavoring to conform your life to it.*

5. *When you have been actively seeking to develop the mind of Christ in all your attitudes.*

6. *When you seek to maintain a listening ear toward God.*

7. *When you gladly take time waiting on God for His guidance.*

8. *When you are teachable and always ready to listen to or consider what mature and spiritual counselors say.*

9. *When you seek to maintain a tender conscience.*

10. *When you keep alert to providential circumstances and open to any step of faith and obedience that God makes clear.*

God Promises Protection From Mistakes

God's promises assure us that a committed, Spirit-filled, prayerful, and watchful Christian need not make a serious mistake. The Lord promises to guide us always (Isa. 58:11). He promises that our Counselor, the Holy Spirit, will always be with us as our indwelling Guide (John 14:17). He promises to caution us whenever we are about to make a mistake in guidance: "Whether you turn to the right or to the left, your ears will hear a voice behind you, saying, 'This is the way; walk in it'" (Isa. 30:21).

It is almost impossible to make a serious mistake in major guidance if you follow the biblical instructions contained in this and other good books. Since God promises to take the responsibility and initiative, you need not be anxious or worried.

How You May Make Mistakes Along the Way

It is possible to be in God's will in most aspects of your life and yet miss God's guidance in specific matters. This can happen because of prayerlessness, carelessness, or a blind spot where you fail to hear the counsel of the Spirit or of others because of some prejudice. (You may not be neutral to what God desires.) It is possible to be slow in sensing God's guidance and thus arrive in the place of God's choosing in a less direct or delayed way. It is possible to be in God's will in general but fail to see and follow through on some of the implications of that will. It is possible to be presumptuous and assume you know the next step because of how God has led thus far. That can be dangerous. God's ways are higher and more varied than your ways.

Signs That You Are Out of God's Will

What if you are walking with God in general obedience but miss God's guidance in some of the details? How can you know if you have made a mistake along the way?

1. Inner restlessness. An inner restlessness may indicate that God is trying to get your attention. Thank God for His faithfulness to you and ask Him to give you peace, or show you the steps you should take now.

2. Perplexity. When you feel perplexed about your course of action and cannot discern the reason, pause and ask God for clarification. Wait until He makes His will clear to you. When you know God guided you to where you are today, make no change until new guidance is equally clear.

3. Disappointment. A pervading, unexplained sense of disappointment may indicate that God is trying to speak to you or restrain you. It may be an indication that He does not approve of a step you are about to take or have just taken.

4. Confusion. A growing and continuing sense of confusion is a strong indication that you may not yet have discerned God's will or are missing His guidance in some way. If there are questions that will not go away, it is time to check whether you have missed God's guidance in some detail. Doubt causes double-mindedness and instability (James 1:6–8).

5. Fanaticism. When you find yourself or others associated with you tending to fanatical extremes, you know this is a red flag of warning. It is a strong danger signal. It indicates that someone has a wrong emphasis or is outside God's will in some pronounced way.

6. Spiritual coolness. When spiritual fervor begins to cool, when spiritual commitments are neglected, when the manifest sense of God's presence begins to be withdrawn, it is time to wake up. Seek God's face anew—somewhere there must be spiritual neglect or confrontation with God's will.

7. Unwise actions. When unwise actions begin to characterize a person or work, when serious mistakes begin to be evident to others outside the group, you know that somewhere people are missing God's will. The will of God is perfect and mature (Rom. 12:2); that which is outside God's will is unwise and foolish (Eph. 5:17). When a person is guided by God, he acts with spiritual, psychological, and social maturity.

You Made a Mistake! Now What?

1. No mistake or sin needs to be final. If you are prepared to commit yourself wholly to God and His will today, He will forgive the past, even where there has been the most serious mistake or sin. He will then take your life where it is today and prepare the most perfect plan possible from this point on. He will not continually chide you about having "second best." He may even help you make up for some of the lost time or opportunities (Joel 2:25).

God still loves you. His grace has a wonderful plan for you, beginning today. Peter failed but was again mightily used by God. John Mark failed Paul and Barnabas, but he was later greatly used by God (he wrote the Gospel of Mark). Paul in time recognized that the past was past and found Mark a useful and needed helper

(2 Tim. 4:11). While not everything that happens is God's highest choice, nothing can happen to finally defeat God's will and plan.

2. God is in sovereign control of your life. He permitted you to use in an unwise way the power of free will that He gave you. You have learned your lesson. When you choose to do His will now, He can again coordinate events and people and include you in His great, overall plan and purpose. Your mistake has not hindered God in ways He cannot overrule.

3. Emphasize God's guidance to you now. Don't spend time mourning over where you missed God's guidance in the past. When you committed your failure to God, He started you anew. You are His child. Rise to your full stature as a forgiven child of God and live for Him today with all your heart and soul. Leave behind what happened outside His will.

Emphasize now what is best within His will. Concentrate on the next details before you. Make a deeper appropriation of His present guidance. Rejoice in the presence of the holy Guide within you and move ahead.

4. Take steps never to repeat your past mistake. Why did you miss those details in God's guidance? Were you spending enough time in God's Word? praying enough? committing yourself and your work to God for His guidance each day? remaining in the close fellowship and counsel of a godly group of Christians? keeping your conscience tender? recognizing and carefully observing God's hand in providence? praising and thanking God for the guidance He was giving you? maintaining a listening ear?

By God's grace, you can become strong where you were formerly weak. You can become watchful where you were negligent. By God's grace and humble obedience on your part, you need not make the same mistake again. If you do, seek all the more never to let it happen the third time. Trust and obey, and move ahead.

мAке guidance your spiritual lifestyle

We have come to the end of a careful study of how God's will and God's guidance are His provision of grace for you. We have seen how God has a great overarching plan of the ages, including His plan for creation, redemption, and the new creation that will continue during the never-ending ages of eternity. Within that glorious plan He has planned for you as His child.

As a totally committed, Spirit-filled child of God you have been provided by God's grace with three primary sources of guidance: the Word of God as your final authority, the Holy Spirit as your indwelling Counselor, and the mind of Christ. As secondary aids in guidance you have God's providence, your conscience, sanctified common sense and wisdom, and the counsel of others.

How can we repeat and sum up the basic steps so that God's promise, "the LORD will guide you always" (Isa. 58:11), can be your experience? How can you make continual guidance your daily experience, your daily joy, your Spirit-filled lifestyle?

Steps to a Guidance Lifestyle

1. Be committed to God's guidance. Make sure that you have made a total surrender of yourself to God and that you continue to affirm this commitment. Be sure you are currently committed to the will of God as far as you understand it. Reaffirm to God daily your desire for His guidance.

2. Live in the fullness of the Spirit. Make sure you have asked and trusted God for the fullness of His Spirit, and live each day in such obedience and spiritual hunger that the Spirit refills and floods you again and again as you expend your spiritual energy in service and face new occasions of need.

3. Seek God's guidance first. Make it your habit to look to God constantly for His guidance, lifting your heart to Him throughout the day for situations small and large. Make God's counsel your priority over human counsel, going to God first and making His word supreme over the word of man. Take the time and effort to seek God's word to you in every major decision.

4. Live thankfully for His guidance. Continually thank God for the privilege of guidance, His promises of guidance, and the Spirit, your ever-present Counselor. Thank Him and rejoice repeatedly in His plan for your life and His guidance throughout your days. Keep lifting your heart in moments of gratitude as you sense His guiding help in the details and commonalities of your day, even in those many situations where He guides and aids without your asking and without your being aware of it until later.

5. Keep listening to God's word to you. Saturate your soul each day in God's Word by systematic, extensive Bible reading. It is more important for you to listen to God than for Him to listen to you. Develop a listening ear that restfully and joyfully expects God to speak at any time.

6. Keep your motive priorities straight. Your primary motive in all you do is to please God, do His will, and extend His kingdom. Your secondary motive in all is to bless others, serve others, and point others toward Christ. Your personal desires, needs, and welfare are important, but must not be your controlling motive. Put God and others before yourself, and God and others will help you.

7. Be active in serving God and living for others. Serve God actively in the place where you are now until He shows you the next step. Watch for opportunities to invest your love, your prayer, and your efforts. Make all your days an investment for eternity. Seek actively to bless as many as you can and to bless as largely as you can. Act on the guidance you receive, being constantly sensitive to the Spirit's timing, enabling, and touch.

8. Be sensitive to the restraints of the Spirit. Remember that the

Spirit will be faithful in leading and restraining you. Trust God to restrain temporarily to keep you in harmony with His timing or plan and to restrain permanently to keep you in His will. Trust Him to restrain you from temptation, mistakes, and danger.

9. Keep humble before God and man. All God's promises are for the humble; nothing blocks God's working more quickly than undue self-confidence or boasting. Apart from God you never have adequate information, adequate common sense, or adequate wisdom. When you have missed details of God's guidance in the past, He has been patient with you. Rejoice in God's guiding goodness to you, but not in the fact that you are the one being guided and used by God. Humbly accept the counsel of others, carefully evaluating it in the light of God's other guiding factors for you.

10. Be willing to take the time to wait on God. Guidance will sometimes come instantly and will at other times require prolonged waiting on God. The waiting time may be necessary because of God's most perfect timing, because you are not yet fully ready, or because the situations or other people are not ready. Beware of impatience or shortcuts in guidance. God's time is always best. You are usually blessed as you wait.

11. Hold steady in times of trial, darkness, or God's silence. All darkness is from Satan, and it will pass. Don't change one step in the dark; wait for God's light to dawn. Don't be surprised at trials, for Satan is opposed to all guided living. Trials will pass, and you will be rewarded here and in eternity. God's silence always has an important reason. It is temporary; God will speak again.

12. Trust God to overrule any mistake. Ask God for forgiveness, and ask Him to help you be more cautious in the future, to profit from your mistake. Ask God to overrule in power and wisdom. God can build even your failures into His overall plan. Relax in His sovereign greatness, His goodness, and His faithfulness.

13. Commit emergencies to God in special prayer. In major decisions where much is hanging in the balance, in sudden crises of major proportions, and in long-standing needs of guidance, resort to extraordinary praying. Enlist the personal prayer of those you know to be strong and wise in prayer. Occasionally a time of prayer and fasting may be the way to discover God's answer. Wherever feasible, arrange a personal prayer retreat for yourself.

14. When you are unsure, but a decision cannot be delayed, trust God and act. God is in sovereign control; the ultimate responsibility in guidance is His. Live in the Spirit; live in guidance; follow the teachings of this book; and move ahead. Don't be immobilized by fear or indecision. Trust all that is in God's hands to work together for His purpose and glory. Relax: God loves you, is with you just now, and takes the responsibility for your life as His obedient child.

Appendix A

YOUR PERSONAL PRAYER RETREAT

Every Spirit-filled believer repeatedly needs the blessing of a personal prayer retreat. It can prove to be one of the most important means to personal spiritual growth, prevailing in prayer, and finding God's guidance in urgent situations. Once you have discovered the blessedness of such a retreat you will want to plan for one at least once or twice a year.

Jesus purposely withdrew from people to have long, uninterrupted personal time with the Father. He took His disciples to less populated places in order to have more fellowship and teaching time with them.

The busier your life or ministry becomes, the more essential it becomes to supplement your customary prayer habits with specially planned times alone with God to saturate your soul in His Word, to worship and praise Him, and to wait in His presence. For many spiritual reasons each Christian needs such times periodically.

How God Honors a Prayer Retreat

1. The Spirit uses a retreat to draw you close to God. We do not know the full meaning of the biblical record that Enoch "walked with God" for three hundred years (Gen. 5:22, 24) and that Noah "walked with God" (Gen. 6:9). The term suggests a steady, continuing, intimate relationship. It undoubtedly involved God's revelation of Himself and His will and their communion with Him.

Whatever was involved, it was very important to the Lord and to these men of God. Each of us needs something of that close relationship with the Lord.

A personal prayer retreat is one of the best means to draw near to God. It gives you the relaxed, uninterrupted time with Him that permits your heart to relate closely to the Lord in love and worship. Communion can become more precious than you have known for some time. You will be able to go from your prayer retreat with a renewed and abiding sense of the Lord's nearness. You will take the blessedness of Christ's presence with you back into your daily life.

2. *The Spirit uses a retreat to refill you with His nature, fullness, and fruit.* If you have made the total surrender of your being to the Lord and have been definitely filled with the Spirit, it is your blessed privilege to be refilled again and again. We read of this in the Book of Acts. It was normal to be filled and refilled.

The 120 were not only filled on the Day of Pentecost, but when threatened by the Sanhedrin, went to prayer and "were all filled with the Holy Spirit" (Acts 4:31). Peter was marked by the fullness before the Sanhedrin (4:8), and Stephen was when he was on trial (7:55). Barnabas was "full of the Holy Spirit" (11:24). Paul was filled in Damascus (9:17) and during the Cyprus ministry (13:9). The disciples at Pisidian Antioch were filled (13:52).

As we live and serve Christ day by day we again and again sense the need of a new refreshing, a new infilling, a new sense of God's Spirit coming upon us and touching us. We do not want to live in the minimum experience of the Spirit. The expression "filled with the Spirit" in Ephesians 5:18 has the present imperative tense in the original Greek. It can be translated "go on being filled with the Spirit" or "be continually filled with the Spirit."

A major way to a new infilling of the Spirit is to spend a longer time communing with the Lord, feasting on His Word, and responding to the Spirit's voice.

3. *The Spirit uses a retreat to give a new and profound sense of guidance.* This is the chief reason for including this appendix in this book. Moses was called up Mount Sinai to a personal retreat with God, and he received detailed guidance for Israel. Elijah in his retreat on Horeb was given guidance as to his successor and the next steps in his ministry (1 Kings 19). Jesus received guidance in

His night of prayer regarding who should be appointed apostles (Luke 6:12–13).

Many of God's children have proved how indispensable it is to have a personal prayer retreat at a time when special guidance is needed. Money could not buy the value I have found in such retreats. At times God gave me guidance in a matter I was not intending to pray about. But I would not have wanted to miss that guidance for anything.

4. *The Spirit uses a retreat to renew His power upon you.* Strength is renewed as you wait "with eager expectation" (the meaning of the Hebrew word translated "wait" in Isaiah 40:31).

"Waiting includes the very essence of a person's being."[1] God's power upon you is renewed as you wait in His presence. God does something in the longer time available in a prayer retreat that does not usually happen in a briefer time of prayer. A renewal of power, a sense of the Spirit's power coming upon you, can have a tremendous impact on your life and ministry.

Charles G. Finney discovered that whenever he began to sense a lessening of God's power, having a time of fasting and prayer for from one to three days always brought a renewal of the Spirit's mighty power. There is an inner renewal of the Spirit that we can experience "day by day" (2 Cor. 4:16). However, we also need the special times of renewal (Acts 3:19). Nothing is more preparatory to this than a personal prayer retreat.

How to Plan Your Prayer Retreat

1. *Find a place where you can be alone.* Find a place to be quiet, undisturbed, and comfortable during the prolonged time of waiting on God. Do you have friends who will be away from home for several days at a time appropriate for you, or with a room somewhat separated from the rest of the house where you can be undisturbed? Is there a summer cabin available to you, or a quiet motel room in a rural environment?

If you plan a retreat for more than a day, you may need to consider a place to lie down and rest. When the weather is good, the

---

[1] R. Laird Harris, ed., *Theological Wordbook of the Old Testament.* 2 vols. (Chicago: Moody Press, 1980), II:791.

advantage of such a place is that you can intersperse your prayer time in the room with a prayer walk out in nature.

2. Select the time for your prayer retreat. Choose a day or days when you can be undisturbed. An official holiday, a weekend, part of your vacation time, or some other free time would be appropriate. You may need to plan well in advance. On other occasions you come to feel the hunger and need of a retreat on shorter notice. You may only be able to schedule daytime hours, or daytime and an evening, or an afternoon and evening.

3. Inform someone. Let someone know where you may be found in case of emergency. It is better if you can be undisturbed by a telephone.

4. Take with you all you will need. You may want a flask of water if none is available. You may want a light snack, some fruit, or other refreshment if yours is not a total fast. Plan to take your reference Bible or a Bible with a concordance, a note pad, and even a hymnbook for singing softly to the Lord or reading some prayer hymns. A flashlight, a cushion or something to kneel on, an alarm clock (especially if you are planning several days of prayer), adequate wraps if the weather is cold, any prayer diary that you will keep—all are things to remember.

Suggestions for the Retreat Time

1. Take a nap if you need one. If you are very exhausted, you may be wise to sleep for an hour and thus be refreshed so you can be at your best. It is spiritual to take a nap when you need it. You may even find it best later during the prayer time to take a brief nap—for example, just after a noon meal on a hot day. Your alarm clock can wake you up.

2. Commit your time to the Lord. Ask Him to take complete control and to guide you throughout the time. Thank Him for the privilege of having a special time with Him.

3. Begin your time with joyful worship. In an emergency you may want to go to intercession first, but when you plan a longer time you should usually begin by rejoicing in the Lord. Read some praise psalms or some hymns from the Book of Revelation (Rev. 4:8–11; 5:6–14; 7:9–12; 14:2–3; 15:2–4; 19:1–7). Read or sing softly a hymn of praise from the hymnal.

4. Feed on God's Word. You will find, as many praying people have found, that it is usually good to begin a time of prayer with listening to God's Word. You are more concerned to hear what God has to say than to talk to Him. Take plenty of time saturating your heart with the Word.

Reading God's Word is one of the best ways to close the door to your unrelated thoughts, your daily concerns and pressures, and thereby be alone with Jesus. Often I have found that when I have a longer time with the Lord, it is very blessed to read twenty-five or even more chapters, especially when reading in the Psalms. Follow the hunger of your heart and the suggestion of the Spirit.

Read to be blessed. Usually you can use other times for more detailed Bible study. If especially helpful insights and thoughts from the Word come to you, feel free to jot them down in your notebook so you won't forget. Then go back to feasting on the Word and rejoicing in God's goodness. You may want to pause and thank the Lord from time to time. You are preparing your heart to sit at Jesus' feet, to love and commune with Him, and later to intercede and perhaps even win prayer battles.

5. Expect God to speak to you. Through His Word or other suggestions that may begin to come to you, God will bring to your attention things important to note down and perhaps pray more about then or later. If extraneous thoughts of something you don't want to forget come to you, jot them down quickly in a separate place, then return to your time with the Lord. As you wait in God's presence, the nearness of the Spirit may bring new and creative suggestions to your mind.

6. Keep thanking the Lord. When you are blessed with your reading of the Word, when the Spirit brings helpful thoughts and suggestions to you, praise and thank the Lord. You may want to spend some time just thinking over God's goodness to you and thanking God one by one for His blessings.

7. Humble yourself before the Lord. Tell the Lord how unworthy you are of all His past goodness and blessing. Tell Him how only He can give the guidance and answers that you need. If He brings past failures to your mind, ask His forgiveness and trust His grace. You may want to note an apology you owe to someone, or some step of reconciliation that you can take.

8. *Put God's kingdom first.* In the Lord's Prayer, Jesus taught us first to pray for the hallowing of God's name, the coming of God's kingdom, and the fulfilling of God's will before we bring our personal petitions. Except in emergencies, it is usually important to pray first for others before we pray for ourselves. It is good to pray for God's kingdom, His church, His cause. Matthew 6:33 assures us that if we seek first God's kingdom and righteousness, He will take care of all our other needs. Put God's agenda first.

9. *Vary your prayer time.* When you have prayed for a while, you may find it good to read again from God's Word. When you have presented your need before the Lord for an extended time, it may be good to praise the Lord again or just wait quietly before Him. Sing a hymn. Take a praise walk or a prayer walk if you can do so without being stopped by others. Vary your prayer posture from time to time—kneel, sit, stand, walk around, just as you feel free and led by the Lord. This will help you to get the most from your prayer time.

10. *Emphasize the personal petitions you have.* You may have one or more special prayer concerns: a need for guidance, the salvation of a loved one, blessing on your church, employment, or more income. After you have put God's kingdom first, you are free to present all your needs before the Lord. But you may feel you should emphasize just one or two during this special prayer time. If you made a list of items for prayer, now is the time to use that list.

11. *Claim God's promise.* Perhaps while you were reading God's Word you saw a promise that seemed to be just for you on this occasion. Perhaps God will bring a promise to your memory. During his night of prayer, Jacob reminded God of His promise (Gen. 32:9). Moses claimed God's promise as he interceded for Israel and presented his own petitions (Exod. 32:13). Like Abraham, take God's promise, place your whole need solidly upon it, and without wavering give praise to God (Rom. 4:20–21). Believe, and you will receive.

12. *Close your prayer time with another time of thanking, praising, and worshiping the Lord.* Thank God for the privilege of this time with Him. Thank Him for the promises that you are claiming. Thank Him for whatever guidance He has given you. Return to your regular duties strengthened, refreshed, and blessed.

Even if you do not have the full answer yet, go trusting the Lord. The beautiful hymn of Miss Goreh of Allahabad, India, titled, "In the Secret of His Presence," closes with these words:

> And whene'er you leave the silence
> of that happy meeting place
> You will surely bear the image
> of the Master in your face.

13. *Make your prayer retreat your secret with the Lord.* It is usually wise not to publicize your time with the Lord. It is your sacred time alone with Jesus. If you need to refer to it because someone tried to contact you, call it a private appointment or engagement. You can mention it in a matter-of-fact way. Perhaps you receive such blessing that at some future time you want to testify to others about it. If you feel God guides you to do so, be careful to give all the glory to the Lord and avoid attracting attention to yourself.

14. *Plan ahead for another precious time alone with Jesus.*

Appendix B

what about a "fleece"?

Have you heard people talk about using a "fleece" to determine God's will?

Judges 6 and 7 relate how God sent "the angel of the LORD" to command Gideon to take leadership and rescue Israel from the pagan nation Midian, which had oppressed Israel seven years. To validate his authority, the angel of the Lord performed a miracle. Remember, this was before there was any canon of Old Testament Scriptures. Moses had written the Pentateuch, but the people did not have copies. The nation was in a leaderless, backslidden condition. There was no prophet to whom Gideon could turn for counsel, and we hear nothing of any godly priests.

Step by step Gideon obeyed the angel of the Lord, and the Holy Spirit came upon him. But the young man longed for some confirmation that God would deliver Israel through him. Gideon placed a wool fleece on the threshing floor and prayed, asking God to drop dew on the fleece that night and to leave the ground all around it dry as a token that He was going to work through him. God granted his request, and in the morning Gideon wrung out a bowlful of water from the fleece. The next night Gideon asked for a second confirmation just the opposite of the night before. That night the fleece was dry and the ground all around it was covered with dew.

Jonathan used a form of "fleece" to obtain guidance for an

assault on a Philistine garrison near Micmash (1 Sam. 14:8–12). The result was that "the Philistines fell before Jonathan" (v. 13).

From these cases some Christians have derived the custom of asking God for some sign to confirm the sense of guidance they have gained through other biblical means and through the inner voice of the Spirit. The "fleece" approach is used by Christians today in words like these:

> "Lord, if You really want me to witness to that man, cause him to stop or walk in my direction."
>
> "Lord, if You want me to put five hundred dollars in the missionary offering, cause my wife to suggest the same amount to me."
>
> "Lord, if You want me to purchase that used car, help the salesman come down five hundred on the price."
>
> "Lord, if You want me to go with that work group to help build the clinic in Ecuador, help my boss to grant permission for me to take time off when the group goes."
>
> "Lord, if You want me to attend that Christian college, guide my church to offer me scholarship aid."

Is this a legitimate way today to test God or to obtain His guidance? Note the following points: God did not suggest this approach to Gideon, but condescended to strengthen his faith by granting his request. There is no indication of any prophet or other leader of Israel using a "fleece" approach to guidance, nor is there a record of its use in the New Testament. Nevertheless, God is sovereign and is free to work as He sees best.

God has undoubtedly honored the "fleece" approach by Christians many times. This is in accord with His constant dealings with man; He uses our vocabulary and illustrations to help us understand His divine truth. Jesus became incarnate to reveal the Father and to provide redemption for us. God often answers unusual prayers in order to help new Christians in pagan lands have Christian faith, and He often performs miracles to prove to non-Christians in pagan lands that Jesus is the living God. God repeatedly accommodates Himself to our human level in order to help us. So there is nothing wrong in asking for a "fleece" if we recognize its limitations.

Suggested Guidelines for Using a "Fleece"

1. There is no clear statement in the Bible approving this method, yet biblical examples show God sometimes accepts it.

2. Today we have the Scriptures, the indwelling Counselor, and God's gracious provisions to guide us, as explained in this book. Today we have centuries of Christian history and biography to give us examples.

3. We should never use a "fleece" for any matter on which the Scripture speaks. God's Word is final.

4. Do not ask God for a "fleece" as the normal way to confirm faith. But occasionally God may be pleased to strengthen your faith in this way.

5. Use a "fleece" only as a supplementary form of guidance, never as a main source of knowing God's will on important issues.

6. Use a "fleece" only after you have sought God's guidance and believe that you know His will. Then, if you feel led to use a "fleece," let it be a supplementary confirmation, an additional means to affirm your choice and to strengthen your faith.

Appendix C

"authority" when your home is non-christian

Remember that each authority person—husband, parent, senior citizen—must be under the authority of Christ. Each is responsible to exercise authority according to the Bible and the example and mind of Christ. How does it affect a situation where the authority person is unsaved, or is a non-Christian in a pagan land?

1. As far as possible, show full respect to the authority person. "Give everyone what you owe him . . . if respect, then respect; if honor, then honor" (Rom. 13:7).

2. God's authority must be followed as far as it is possible to do so. If the authority person commands something contrary to the Word of God—immoral, unjust, or below Christian standards—God's authority always supersedes the authority person.

3. Explain to the authority person that you love, honor, pray for, and obey him in all other things, but you have to obey God rather than man (Acts 5:29). In this instance you regretfully yet humbly must disobey and put God first.

4. It may be wise to ask God's help to escape to a place of safety, if there is such available, in some extreme cases, as where life is in danger (perhaps a convert in some non-Christian societies).

5. Some decisions may need to be deferred. For example, a decision might not be made in the matter of baptism until the Christian reaches the age of majority, especially where government rules forbid baptism of a minor.

6. *When a person reaches the age of majority in a culture where extreme respect is shown to parents, the Christian has the right to make his own decisions and live his own life even if the authority person does not approve.* In some cases, in an effort to still win the authority person to Christ, God may guide to defer some of the normal Christian practices (such as regular attendance at Christian worship) for a time.

7. *Continue to show great love, respect, and a Christlike spirit to the authority person in all situations.* Continue to pray for the salvation of that person, and ask God's guidance in how to show or give witness and how to be a blessing to the person.

BIBLIOGRAPHY

Barclay, William. *The Gospel of John*. Vol. 2 of *The Daily Study Bible*. Edinburgh: Saint Andrew Press, 1955.

Benner, David G., ed. *Baker Encyclopedia of Psychology*. Grand Rapids: Baker Book House, 1985.

Brown, Colin, gen. ed. *The New International Dictionary of New Testament Theology*. 3 vols. Grand Rapids: Zondervan Publishing House, 1967.

Bruce, F. F. *The Epistle to the Ephesians*. Old Tappan, N.J.: Fleming H. Revell Company, 1961.

————. *The Epistles to the Colossians, to Philemon, and to the Ephesians*. The New International Commentary on the New Testament, edited by F. F. Bruce. Grand Rapids: Wm. B. Eerdmans Publishing Co., 1984.

Carter, Charles W., gen. ed. *The Wesleyan Bible Commentary*. 7 vols. Grand Rapids: Wm. B. Eerdmans Publishing Co., 1968.

Cumming, J. Elder. *Through the Eternal Spirit*. Stirling, Scotland: Stirling Tract Enterprise; London: Marshall, Morgan & Scott, 1937.

Ferguson, Sinclair B. *Discovering God's Will*. Carlisle, Pa.: The Banner of Truth Trust, 1982.

Friesen, Garry, with J. Robin Maxson. *Decision Making and the Will of God*. Portland, Oreg.: Multnomah Press, 1980.

Gaebelein, Frank E., gen. ed. *The Expositor's Bible Commentary*. 12 vols. Grand Rapids: Zondervan Publishing House, 1984.

Green, Michael. *I Believe in the Holy Spirit*. Grand Rapids: Wm. B. Eerdmans Publishing Co., 1975.

Harper, A. F., chm. *Beacon Bible Commentary*. 10 vols. Kansas City, Mo.: Beacon Hill Press, 1969.

Harris, R. Laird, ed. *Theological Wordbook of the Old Testament*. 2 vols. Chicago: Moody Press, 1980.

Howard, J. Grant, Jr. *Knowing God's Will—and Doing It!* Grand Rapids: Zondervan Publishing House, 1976.

Knapp, Martin Wells. *Impressions*. Cincinnati: Revivalist Publishing House, 1892.

Little, Paul E. *Affirming the Will of God*. Downers Grove, Ill.: InterVarsity Press, 1971.

Macaulay, J. C. *Life in the Sp:.it*. Grand Rapids: Wm. B. Eerdmans Publishing Co., 1955.

Morris, Leon. *Spirit of the Living God*. London: Inter-Varsity Fellowship, 1960.

Murray, Andrew. *God's Will: Our Dwelling Place*. Formerly *Thy Will Be Done*. Springdale, Pa.: Whitaker House, 1982.

_____. *The Spirit of Christ*. Minneapolis: Bethany Fellowship, 1979.

Murray, John. *The Epistle to the Romans*. 2 vols. *The New International Commentary on the New Testament*, edited by F. F. Bruce. Grand Rapids: Wm. B. Eerdmans Publishing Co., 1968.

Ogilvie, Lloyd John. *Discovering God's Will in Your Life*. Eugene, Oreg.: Harvest House Publishers, 1982.

Oswalt, John N. *The Book of Isaiah, Chs. 1–39. The New International Commentary Series*. Grand Rapids: Wm. B. Eerdmans Publishing Co., 1986.

Smith, M. Blaine. *Knowing God's Will*. Downers Grove, Ill.: InterVarsity Press, 1979.

Stauffer, Joshua. *"When He Is Come."* Berne, Ind.: Light and Hope Publications, 1948.

Strong, James. *Strong's Exhaustive Concordance*. Reprint. Grand Rapids: Baker Book House, 1982.

Tasker, R. V. G., gen. ed. *Tyndale New Testament Commentaries*. 20 vols. London: The Tyndale Press, 1960.

Taylor, Richard S., ed. *Beacon Dictionary of Theology*. Kansas City, Mo.: Beacon Hill Press, 1983.

Thompson, Fred P. *The Holy Spirit: Comforter, Teacher, Guide*. Wheaton, Ill.: Victor Books, 1978.

Vine, W. E. *The Expanded Vine's Dictionary of New Testament Words*. Minneapolis: Bethany House Publishers, 1984.

_____. *The Epistles to the Philippians and Colossians*. London: Oliphants Ltd., 1955.

Warne, Frank W. *A Prayer-answering Christ*. Madras: Madras Publishing House, 1932.

Weatherhead, Leslie D. *The Will of God*. Nashville: Abingdon Press, 1944.

Wiley, H. Orton. *The Epistle to the Hebrews*. Kansas City, Mo.: Beacon Hill Press, 1959.

Wood, A. Skevington. *Life by the Spirit*. Formerly *Paul's Pentecost*. Grand Rapids: Zondervan Publishing House, 1964.

Woolsey, Andrew. *Duncan Campbell*. London: Hodder and Stoughton, 1974.

index